WITCH-HUNT:
THE ASSIGNMENT OF BLAME

WITCH-HUNT:
THE ASSIGNMENT OF BLAME

Dr. Clifton Wilcox

Copyright © 2012 by Dr. Clifton Wilcox.

ISBN: Softcover   978-1-4691-8112-7
            Ebook   978-1-4691-8113-4

All rights reserved. No part of this book may be reproduced or transmitted in any form or by any means, electronic or mechanical, including photocopying, recording, or by any information storage and retrieval system, without permission in writing from the copyright owner.

This book was printed in the United States of America.

To order additional copies of this book, contact:
Xlibris Corporation
1-888-795-4274
www.Xlibris.com
Orders@Xlibris.com

Table of Contents

AUTHORS NOTE		9
CHAPTER ONE:	*Understanding the Puritans*	11
CHAPTER TWO:	*The Role of the Scapegoat*	19
CHAPTER THREE:	*Salem: The Beginning of the Nightmare*	21
CHAPTER FOUR:	*Setting the Stage*	23
CHAPTER FIVE:	*Enter George Burroughs*	27
CHAPTER SIX:	*The Witch-Hunt*	31
CHAPTER SEVEN:	*What say the Afflicted?*	33
CHAPTER EIGHT:	*Closing of the Witch-Hunt*	42

> Quick to judge
> Quick to anger
> Slow to understand
> Ignorance and prejudice
> And fear walk hand in hand . . .
> -Rush (1981)

Books by Dr. Clifton Wilcox:

Scapegoat: Targeted for Blame

Groupthink: An Impediment to Success

Bias: The Unconscious Deceiver

AUTHORS NOTE

The witch panic at Salem in 1692 was not just the result of a miasma of circumstances coincidentally falling into place but something that was also consciously and deliberately kindled, fueled, and manipulated. A main difference between Salem and previous New England witch trials was in its virulence, magnitude, and scope. This author can only sum up the Salem episode in relation to other New England witch trials as analogous to the difference between a fire that occurs naturally from a lightning strike followed by the rainstorm that puts it out and an inferno set deliberately in several places on a windy day in dry season to inflict maximum damage.

CHAPTER ONE

Understanding the Puritans

The Puritans of Salem were a population that had suffered religious persecution in the Old World. They fled to America for the sole purpose of establishing their religion. Having endured persecution in England, the Puritans had little toleration and began persecuting others who held different religious beliefs in America.[1] The Puritans believed Puritanism was the one and only true religion and were the closest to God.[2]

The Puritans lived in a theocratic society. Ministers were usually the main officers and administrators of the government. An individual who was not in good standing with the church had limited rights and would not be allowed to vote or hold an office. Those individuals who continued not be in good standing with the church were punished through excommunication which involved banishment, shunning, and shaming. Excommunication ultimately resulted in the individual and his or her family to lose all property rights.[3]

While belief in the devil and witchcraft was not isolated to any branch of Christianity, certain tenets made the Puritans of New England particularly susceptible to belief in the Devil and witches.[4] The Puritan's belief system stressed that an active evil force was operating with the goal of obliterating God's kingdom on earth.[5] The Puritans personified this force as the Devil. The Puritans held a strong belief that the Devil was principally interested in unleashing an assault on them, since they were God's new chosen people.[6]

The Puritan obsession with evil was linked with their relentless desire to affirm their superiority. Their domination of external realities reflected the domination of their inner lives, carried out for the sake of purity. The *Doctrine of the Elect* emphasized superiority.[7] This doctrine stated that at birth or later an individual might be chosen by God to become one of the Elect and that this Elect would receive God's grace and eternal salvation.[8] Puritans lived righteous lives and to constantly prepare to be an Elected member, if the day came. The Puritans held a belief that those who were never Elected would not and could not be saved.[9]

The Puritan logic was simple, if God could Elect certain people to be saved, then the Devil could select others to be bewitched.[10] Here, the Puritans were extra-vigilant about identifying witches and those who consorted and joined the Devil's ranks. The Puritans held that once an individual had entered into a covenant with the Devil, that individual would persistently attack the innocent.[11] The Puritans held that that witches could enter into any upstanding member and devout Puritan's body without him or her knowing it.[12] They also widely held that witches could assume the shape of innocent people and then torment others. The tormented ones would then accuse innocent individuals of being witches; and that the falsely accused would be brutally and unjustly admonished by the community. This was the Devil's grand scheme and this was how the Devil would disrupt Puritan society.[13]

The Puritans' literal interpretation of the Bible, according to Levin, condoned their harsh treatment of witches: Exodus 22:18 "Thou shalt not suffer a witch to live."[14] Yet, most Puritans believed that once a person confessed to being a witch, he or she became free from those bounds.[15] The first step in the process of being saved was an open confession of one's sins. Another faction of the church, however, believed that confessing to being a witch would eternally damn a person. Many innocent people accused of witchcraft who might otherwise have falsely confessed in order to save their lives, therefore, refused to do so because they believed that even a false confession would result in eternal damnation.[16]

Historians have noted, moreover, that the Puritans' concept of the Devil grew out of their acceptance of the *Doctrine of Original Sin*, which informed them that they were "worms, dogs, potential colleagues of the Devil until the grace of God . . . poured into them."[17] The Puritans held a strong belief that they were tainted by evil at birth. This was further supported by ministers whose sermons depicted them as always being on the verge of damnation. The Puritan society, at large, were seen as highly prone to becoming witches. Puritans believed that they needed to vigilantly purify themselves and their community of this inherent evil so they could accept God's grace and become one of the Elect.[18] Purifying themselves and their community meant living austere lives characterized by hard work, prayer, confession, and penance.[19]

The Situation in Salem

The Puritans' unique historical situation generated immense anxiety. This historical situation included: their cultivation of moral superiority as a strategy for challenging the powerful British aristocracy; their resultant persecution and exile; the grandiose and paranoid traits linked with their ideology of being the chosen people; their struggle for survival in the ominous American wilderness; the growing disparity between their fanatical ideology and the reality of liberty both for the Puritans in England and for the population of the American colonies; and various local social and political disputes which were acute at the time of the Salem outbreak.[20] When the Puritans could no longer suppress this anxiety, it began to emerge in the form of increasing attacks upon what they saw as the devil.

Prior to the Witch Trials

The Puritans' work group focused on meeting basic survival needs. They sought food, water, and physical protection. They strived for unity to fend off ideological or material enemies. The theocratic nature of Puritan society can be viewed as a specialized work group. Prior to the witch trials, the theocracy appears to have coped with basic assumption phenomena in a manner that enabled the work group to function.[21] The theocracy responded to a build-up of primitive anxiety within the group by allowing for shifts between the three basic assumptions. [22] The doctrines adopted and established by the specialized work group express basic assumption phenomena. These beliefs helped the community maintain a sense of unity. Pairing is evident in the Puritans' belief in the *Doctrine of the Elect* and their belief that the Kingdom of God would arrive at the millennium.[23] Dependency is shown in the literal interpretation of the Bible and the belief in one God who is relied on for salvation. Lastly, fight-flight appears to have been manifested in the flight from the Old World in response to persecution.[24] It is also evident in Puritans' complete acceptance of the *Doctrine of Original Sin*, which required them to fight against evil in order to purify themselves and their community.[25] As well as it is evident in the intolerance of anyone whose beliefs differed from those of the Puritans.[26]

There are a number of frameworks that can be extended to take into account the historical component of the Puritans' anxiety.[27] The historical situation of the Puritans, which centered around and involved them in a variety of disputes, threats, and challenges to their ideology, engendered great anxiety.[28] Yet, the Puritan character structure was rooted in the denial of impulses through their projection onto external phenomena. In the Puritan community, hostilities and desires needed to be tracked down and expunged from their consciousness.[30] In the New World, expressions of liberty such as the freedom to practice other religions were a terrifying threat. When the community could no longer suppress it, therefore, the Puritans' massive anxiety burst forth in a group hysteria and psychosis.[31] As suggested by Hazell, low-status community members frequently become repositories for what is seen as dirty, unseemly, ignorant, and foolish.[32] These low-status members act as containers for what is thought to be shameful, uncomfortable, and undesirable.[33] In Salem, those of the lowest classes and thus the most vulnerable—women, the elderly, and the poor—became targets for the projection of anxiety and hostility in the guise of being 'witches'.[34] Here, the Puritans could finally release the intense psychic impulses which had been pent up for so long. In the act of destroying these 'witches', the higher status Puritans could obliterate the anxiety within themselves.[35]

Initially, the specialized work group was relied on in an attempt to cope with these anxieties ritualistically through fasting and prayer. Yet, anxieties of the population could no longer be contained through ritual, however, when word of the "witch" got out. At this point, the work group function of the main group may have become ineffective. Once the work group had been disrupted, shifts between the three basic assumptions most likely occurred, depending on the intensity and nature of the emotions seeking expression at any given time.[36]

The flight-fight assumption appears to have become more deeply translated into the reification of the Devil.[37] An intense need emerged to wage a concrete battle against the Devil and his followers in Salem. By way of this basic assumption, unmitigated hatred could be expressed toward the socially sanctioned enemy that was the Devil and his followers. Because the enemy was socially sanctioned, group members could avoid guilt in response to their open expression of vengeance toward the accused.[38] A number of Salem's leader believed in vigorously prosecuting the witches, that may have served as the basic assumption group. Many of those attacked by the group may have been targeted because they possessed characteristics not condoned by the larger group. The first three individuals prosecuted were likely candidates. According to Levin: "Tituba was a West Indian and a conjurer; Sarah Good was a destitute, wizened, pipe-smoking hag; Sarah Osborne had been suspected of immorality . . ."[39] Panic became evident in that the work group was not designed to cope with a direct attack by the Devil. The fear and rage characteristic of the group's panicked state may have become split off and placed in the 'afflicted' girls, who in turn, acted out this affect through their 'fits' and panic attacks.[40] Processing the emotions associated with panic through the 'afflicted' "fits," where the girls may have unburdened the larger group, allowing it to obliterate the enemy in a methodical and seemingly emotionless way.[41]

Puritans Social Defenses.

Another perspective, one could presume that many of those accused of witchcraft most likely threatened the Puritans' social defense structure, and were therefore easily targeted for the projection of impulses.[42] The Puritans instituted social defense structures that institutionalize a set of primitive defenses, such as splitting and projective identification.[43] These Puritan defenses were institutionalized and codified in religious beliefs. The use of splitting, as an example, was clearly evident in the Puritan belief that a continual war waged between Satan and God.[44] These external battles between God (all good) and Satan (all bad) clearly manifested an internal psychic split endured by the Puritans in a desperate attempt to keep the good object untainted by dangerous temptations and impulses.[45] Those Puritans who failed to conform were viewed as bad and rejected; and at times ostracized by the community.

This conformity required Puritan members to attend church regularly, interpret the bible literally, and demonstrate an extensive knowledge of catechism; which were a set of instructions in the principles of Christianity using a series of questions and answers that tested religious knowledge.[46] Many of those who were accused of witch-craft were unsuccessful in catechism or failed to conform to these standards. The Puritans found that these individual would have threatened the communities social defense structure, eliciting the very impulses the Puritans sought to repress. As an example, John Proctor was convicted partially on the grounds that he did not attend church regularly.[47] The Puritan elite "piled on" more charges based on his expressed skepticism about the whole idea of witchcraft.[48] This was viewed as questioning the scriptures, in which the Puritans held as a grave crime. In another example, the Puritan elite charged and convicted Goody Osborne largely on the fact that she did not know the ten-commandments.[49] The Puritan community had found that these behaviors were especially unsettling since they questioned the dangerous, repressive mentality on which the Puritan society was based.

Those accused of being witches elicited behaviors and feelings that were linked with freedom, diversity, sexuality, and hostility; sensations and emotions that the Puritans took monumental strides to suppress.[50] The Puritan ideology was meant to dominate and silence the self. These denied feelings were then projected onto others, where they are attacked as the enemy. The Puritan elite could feel pure, strong, and morally right if everything they had feared in themselves since childhood could be attributed to the witches.[51]

The *Doctrine of the Elect* and the *Doctrine of Original Sin* institutionalize projective identification.[52] The *Doctrine of the Elect* enables members to split off the good and righteous parts of the group and place them in the Elect members of the community for safe keeping; where it was believed that the Elect received God's grace.[53] Once the good parts of the group were inside these members, they felt protected forever because the Elect could do no wrong and were guaranteed by God to have eternal salvation.[54]

In general, the Elect could not and would not be subject to accusations of witchcraft. Based on the *Doctrine of Original Sin*, group members who were not Elect were tainted by original sin and could therefore be viewed as containers for the immoral and wickedness of the group.[55] These Non-Elect members had to submit to the ritualistic cycle of publicly confessing their sins, repenting, and finally performing an act of penance to have any hope of being saved. Once Non-Elect members were charged with being witches, the accused were treated in such a way as to obtain verification of the fact, usually by obtaining a confession through torture.[56] If those accused conformed to the ritualistic cycle and confessed to being a witch, repented, and did penance, they could be saved.[57] Those who refused to confess, however, threatened the social defense structure. They could therefore be used as scapegoats without guilt.

The Splitting of Good and Bad

Prior to the Salem witch trials, the Puritan community used ritualized religious system as a way to reinforce those defenses that are typical of the depressive position, which include obsessive tendencies, mania, and denial. The Puritans accusations of witchcraft appeared to suggest a shift to an emphasis on the paranoid-schizoid position. This shift included the use of more primitive defenses such as splitting and projective identification.[58] Yet, following the trials, the Puritan community seemed to have been a reintegration of group processes and therefore a lessened reliance on paranoid/schizoid defenses.[59]

Before the trials, the Non-Elect community members were believed to be tainted by the original sin that focused on an obsessive struggle to repair the damage through prayer, hard work, and the meticulous conformity to the mandates of their faith.[60] Puritan Ministers encouraged group members to confess, repent, and perform ritualized acts of penance. The Puritans were caught up in a constant battle to repair the damage through obsessive repetition of the confession, repentance, and penance cycle. Additionally, mania and denial were evident in the notion that there were Elect members of the community. The Elect members represented idealized objects who had been magically repaired through God's grace.[61] The group denied the mortality of these members who were viewed as saved forever. The collective denial of the fallibility of the Elect suggests that the Puritan ideal is that once they have received God's grace, they could do no wrong. The depressive line of defense appeared to dominate the group functioning up until the series of disturbing events; which led to a build-up of annihilation and persecutory anxiety.[62] This build-up triggered a collective shift to a paranoid-schizoid way of processing information.[63]

The daily primitive anxieties that the Puritan community struggled with could now be disposed of through projective identification. The Puritan community projected bad internal objects and impulses onto lesser members of the community who would then absorb these parts and contain them.[64] Once objectified in the accused, these bad parts could more easily be controlled by the group through the elicitation of confessions. The bad objects and impulses could then be given back to the group in a partially metabolized and thus more tolerable form.[65] Yet, if the accused lesser member refused to confess to witchcraft, the community at large could symbolically rid itself of the bad objects and impulses by executing the witch.[66]

Projective identification became more evident in the "fits" that the 'afflicted' girls had presented. At times, these fits were portrayed as most violent and out-of—control. Additionally, there were moments when the 'afflicted' girls would scream in terror and make strange and bizarre sounds. It might have been that the girls served as containers for the rage and terror experienced by the larger group.[67] The 'fits' had been characterized and in way served as verification to the group that the girls did undeniably held the split off bad parts.[68] The girls would then transfer and deflect these bad impulses by placing them in those whom they accused of witchcraft. The accused person, in theory, would absorb the impulses, or deflect them. An example of an accused witch deflecting is evident in the testimony of the servant Tituba. Tituba admitted to being a witch and begged for the congregations forgiveness.[69] She then, in turn, accused two other community members of witchcraft.[70]

Puritan witch-hunting also indicated splitting. The group ignored any benevolent acts that an accused individual engaged in prior to being charged with witchcraft.[71] Once deemed a witch, the individual was viewed by the group as all evil, and the devil incarnate.[72] The group split off any aspect of the individual's past identity.

Once the threat of execution ended, the group could begin operating from the depressive position. A more humanistic and interactive group process enabled members to reflect on what was taking place. The repressive social outlook underlying the witch—hunt began to break down.[73] A prohibition against the use of spectral evidence and the testimony of the bewitched may have led the entire community to reflect more rationally on what had happened.[74] Once the persecutions were questioned, community members began to perceive those who were accused as whole objects.[75] This was suggested by several members of the jury who publicly expressed remorse for potentially convicting innocent people after the executions were stopped.[76] Confessions by various parties suggested an attempt to repair the objects that had been so brutally injured. Community members began to grieve, over participating and being a part of the process of what had occurred. For over a ten year period following the trials, according to Boyer, Salem officials and residents tried obsessively to repair the damaged objects through numerous public apologies and ultimately by awarding sums of money to the descendants of accused witches.[77] Because the group members were more open, more reflective, and able to emotionally process, basic assumptions could no longer derail the group process.

CHAPTER TWO

The Role of the Scapegoat

The term scapegoat is used to describe individuals who are identified with evil, blamed for the misfortunes of the family or communal group, and seen as deviants from the culturally defined norm.[1] The scapegoat is generally innocent of the mistakes or crimes of which he or she has been accused. Its assigned fault lies in being different from those placing the blame. The scapegoat's differences may show up in various ways: homosexuals, foreigners, the disabled, people of color, those too strong, too weak, or who display a strong instinctive nature—even the *avant-garde* scientist or artist draw blame and ostracism.[2]

The ancient and universal practice of scapegoating originally served to transfer the people's sense of sin to a condemned human, animal, or object, keep further persecution or punishment at bay, and bring about a new contact with a higher spiritual order of life.[3] Today, the practice of allocating blame continues so that the people's sense of virtue and control can remain intact.[4] Arthur Colman, a Jungian analyst and clinical professor at the University of California, San Francisco, said that the scapegoat is the most pervasive myth of group life:

> The basis of the scapegoat myth is this: the group is not to blame for its problems, its bad feelings, its pain, its defeats. These are the responsibility of a particular individual or subgroup—the scapegoat—who is perceived as being fundamentally different from the rest of the group and must be excluded or sacrificed in order for the group to survive and remain whole.[5]

Those who scapegoat others seem driven to rid themselves of any sense of blame or wrong-doing. To understand this phenomenon, it is important to look at the connection between the shadow, feelings of guilt, and the role of the scapegoat.

When people feel a sense of duty to live a certain way, in accordance with the customs of a family or the rules of an agency for instance, and the person is convinced of the earnestness of these duties, perceived personal shortcomings can shatter the person's illusion of being perfect. In Jungian psychology, the perceived shortcomings are known as the shadow.[6] Jungian analyst Sylvia Perera said that the unease associated with shadow characteristics is at the root of scapegoating:

> In Jungian terms, scapegoating is a form of denying the shadow of both man and God. What is seen as unfit to conform with the ego ideal, or with the perfect goodness of God, is repressed, denied, or split off and made unconscious.[7]

In large part, the ego ideal has taken on the moral code of society that in turn has been derived from the word of God. In the Judeo-Christian tradition of Western culture, God is viewed as an external deity and seen as being all good.[8] It has become imperative that instinctual behavior or urges not of God's choosing and thus considered a sin—being highly aggressive, greedy, or sensual for example—be eliminated. The presence of these behaviors—the shadow material—can evoke unbearable feelings of guilt, and within some religious models, fear of eternal damnation. The scapegoaters need to create the scapegoats and make them responsible for their own perceived shortcomings. The shadow material can be seen in projection, and by using a scapegoat, the person's feelings of guilt for not having lived up to the standards or morals of the collective can be alleviated.

CHAPTER THREE

Salem: The Beginning of the Nightmare

On an ill-fated day in 1692, a harmless childhood game set in motion a chain of events that would forever make Salem, Massachusetts, infamous in American history. In the kitchen of Reverend Samuel Parris, a household slave was telling the fortunes of four young girls by lekanomancy, in which an egg-white is dropped into a glass of water; the patterns that are formed are interpreted as signs of the future.[1] The girls, hoping to see the faces of their future husbands, instead saw the shape of a coffin—an evil omen. In fear, they screamed, exposing their forbidden game to Reverend Parris. To avoid punishment, the girls threw themselves onto the floor, claiming to be bewitched.[2] The Reverend immediately called for the village doctor who diagnosed the girls as possessed by evil spirits of the invisible world.[3]

As news of the possession spread, the villagers prayed. However, the girls remained possessed and their diabolic behavior spread to others.[4] Unable to stop this epidemic, Magistrate John Hathorne proclaimed that this sinister behavior was not the work of some unseen evil forces, but was the demonic work of the Devil and his witches who were living in Salem.[5] As a result, has proclamation transformed the Salem witch-craze from allegations of maleficium—using witchcraft to do harm to a neighbor to accusations of diabolism, where some in the community had made a pact with the Devil to destroy the Puritan society.[6]

Horrified, the townspeople demanded that the girls name the witches who had possessed them. Accusations came in droves. Within a month, three hundred and four persons were accused, imprisoned, or tried for the crime of witchcraft.[7] On the morning of August 19, 1692, on Gallows Hill, nineteen of those convicted of witchcraft, including the Reverend George Burroughs, were hanged.[8] Although the most neglected player of the Salem witchcraft trails,

George Burroughs has the distinction of being the only Puritan minister and accused New England witch to be tried, convicted, and executed for being the leader of the witches and the Devil incarnate.[9]

Was George Burroughs simply another unfortunate victim or the ultimate scapegoat? The following chapters will use credible sources to piece together the puzzle that will show George Burroughs fulfilled the New England clergy's and Salem magistrates' obsessions with finding a scapegoat; thereby proving their claims of a demonic conspiracy to destroy New England and justifying their witch-cleansing methods.

CHAPTER FOUR

Setting the Stage

For three hundred years, historians of witchcraft have remained steadfast in two separate groups regarding the nature of Salem witchcraft trials; one group has defined the outbreak as maleficium, the other as diabolism.[1] Yet both camps have continued to disregard George Burroughs. His case is often buried in the footnotes of the witchcraft chronicles.

The debate over the nature of the Salem witch craze and neglect of George Burroughs started when contemporary figures such as Increase Mather, Cotton Mather, Deodat Lawson, Francis Dane, and Robert Calef disagreed. The Mathers and Lawson argued that the Salem epidemic expressed a physical manifestation of the Devil's existence.[2] Lawson, in *A Brief and True Narrative* (1692), wrote, "Satan endeavors . . . to make his kingdom and administration resemble those of our Lord Jesus Christ."[3] Firmly convinced that witches lived among them and the trails constituted a legitimate method of purging them, these men also came to the conclusion that George Burroughs was not only the leader of the witches but the Devil himself.[4] Increase Mather claimed Burroughs was "guilty of the . . . crimes of witchcraft,"[5] while Cotton Mather declared "our God miraculously sent in five Andover witches . . . all agreeing in Burroughs being their ring-leader."[6]

In the late eighteenth and early nineteenth centuries, witchcraft historians began developing theories regarding the causes of the Salem witchcraft trials. Still, they remained divided over the nature and continued to overlook the pivotal role of George Burroughs. Historian Sarah Loring Bailey, in *Historical Sketches of Andover*, argued that although most of the New England witches were females accused of maleficium, in times of extreme social turmoil more males were accused of diabolism than historians have acknowledged.[7] To prove this assertion, she chronicled the trials of accused males in the New

England witch-hunts of 1673, 1675, 1676, 1689, and the 1692 Andover outbreak, in which more than half the forty-three accused were men.[8] Still, Bailey considered the Salem and Andover witch-hunts based on maleficium and down played the significance of Burroughs, although he was the only New England witch to be executed for diabolism.[9]

In the 1970s, interest in Salem witchcraft increased. Historians Paul Boyer and Steven Nissenbaum, co-authors of *Salem Possessed*, developed a line of inquiry for American witch-craft that followed the path of British historians Alan MacFarlane and Keith Thomas, claiming that witch hunts served as a function of resolving family and neighborhood conflicts, and explaining strange illnesses, unusual accidents, and sudden deaths.[10] Boyer and Nissenbaum mapped the social and physical geography of Salem Village and uncovered a longstanding feud over land between two families, the Putnams and the Porters.[11] The two theorized that the Putnams had accused the Porters and their neighbors of witchcraft to get their land; New England law decreed that when an individual was accused of witchcraft their land was immediately confiscated and put on public auction.[12] Yet these historians ignored Burroughs in their study as he was neither a Salem resident nor related to anyone in Massachusetts; thus, he seemed outside local grievances.

One hundred years after Bailey examined accused male-witches, scholars began to focus on accused female-witches. Joseph Klaits in *Servants of Satan*, and Carol Karlsen in *The Devil in the Shape of a Woman*, claimed that the Salem witch-hunts resulted from a patriarchal fear of women.[13] Klaits stressed that most of the accused female witches practiced midwifery, while Karlsen pointed out that the majority of the accused women had threatened the patriarchal structure by either becoming land-owners or beggars; wealthy women were threats to this male-dominated society's control over finances, and poor women were visible reminders of its economic unbalance.[14] These scholars overlooked Burroughs as he was neither a female, a midwife, nor an economic threat.

In a more recent inquiry into the Salem witchcraft trails, David Hall, in *Witch-Hunting in Seventeenth Century New England*, maintained that the term 'witch' functioned as a label to control or punish someone.[15] Puritans "applied the term to any quarrelsome or 'difficult' people, or to those who somehow trespassed on the mores of the community."[16] Hall used the Burroughs' case as an example of 'witch-labeling,' but did not expound upon the man's central role in the Salem witch-craze.[17] He simply grouped Burroughs with the accused witches who were charged with arguing, missing church, or not baptizing their children.

On the other side of the debate over the nature of the Salem outbreak, the claims that the accusations were fraudulent and the trials wrong, started when such seventeenth-century figures as Reverend Francis Dane and Robert

Calef declared that innocent people were being hanged.[18] Dane, the Puritan minister at Andover, told his congregation that the hunts would continue "if the accusations of children and others . . . shall be received against persons of good fame."[19] Calef, the greatest critic of the trials, proclaimed that the clergy and magistrates were allowing innocent blood to be shed.[20] In *More Wonders of the Invisible World*, Calef wrote "as long as the clergy and Court granted the Devil such great powers . . . God will be daily dishonored."[21] Although Calef used the Burroughs' case as an example of the innocent being hanged for a crime based on superstition, neither he nor the other critics of the witchcraft trails viewed Burroughs as a scapegoat.[22]

In the 1940's, however, scholars developing a psychological interpretation of witchcraft theorized that the Salem witch-craze was an aberration based upon mass delusions. Marion L. Starkey, in *The Devil in Massachusetts*, wrote that the Salem tragedy was started by some little girls trying to escape punishment by displaying "deviant behaviors that spread into a mass delusion."[23] Twenty years later, Elliot Woodward supported Starkey's argument in *Records of Salem Witchcraft Copied from the Original Documents*, adding that it was specifically the Puritan clergy who spread the delusions.[24] In 1983, Chadwick Hansen focused on the mass delusion at Andover, claiming that the New England witch-craze ignited in Salem but exploded in Andover when eight delusional "witches" testified that George Burroughs, a man they had never met, was their leader.[25] These historians claimed that the witch-hunts were based on mass delusions, but have not examined the critical link between the delusions of Andover witches and the authorities' selection of Burroughs as the root of evil.

As the study of Salem witchcraft expanded, some historians re-evaluated the religious nature of the Salem tragedy. Perry Miller, in *The New England Mind*, concluded that it was the clergy's excessive zeal to maintain a theocratic society that created the Salem witch-craze.[26] Cotton Mather's biographer, Kenneith Silverman, in *The Life and Times of Cotton Mather*, also attributed the Salem tragedy to the clergy, claiming that they uncharacteristically sacrificed a Puritan minister, George Burroughs, to control a disintegrating Puritan community.[27] However, these historians focused more on the accusers than the accused, leaving critical questions unanswered: How could a Puritan minister be convicted of witchcraft, when it as believed that a man of the cloth could not be corrupted by the Devil? How did Cotton Mather's biblical description of the Devil ultimately convince the Court that Burroughs and Satan were the same entity?

By the 1970s and 1980s, more historians began viewing the Salem witch-craze as an aberration.[28] For example, John Demos stated that the Salem witch-hunt resulted from "abnormal social and family hostilities that pitted young girls against middle-aged women."[29] He claimed that when a culture imposes strict rules of social behavior and religious beliefs upon the young, witchcraft accusations against authority figures often occur.[30] To prove this point, he charted the testimonies in the Salem transcripts, showing that most of the accusers were young girls and their victims adult women.[31] However, he neglected the importance of the accusers' increasing hostility toward authority when they claimed a Puritan minister, the ultimate authority figure, was the 'above' conjuror.

In more recent witchcraft inquiry, Enders Robinson in *The Devil Discovered*, devoted an entire chapter to George Burroughs.[32] He used this case to argue that Salem was not a typical New England witch-hunt, but a conspiracy of zealous clergymen and greedy land owners that was sanctioned by the magistrates.[33] Unfortunately, Ender focused more on Cotton Mather's persecution of the witches than on Burroughs as a scapegoat.

While the debate over the nature of the Salem outbreak has continued, the inquiry on George Burroughs has remained stagnant. The rest of this book will not rehash or explore the nature of the Salem witchcraft trails, but focus on why the clergy and magistrates singled out George Burroughs and used him as the ultimate scapegoat. The idea is to understand Burroughs and his central role in the Salem witchcraft trails. In order to do that, we must expose the man and the events that led up to his trial, conviction, and eventually his execution.

CHAPTER FIVE

Enter George Burroughs

Who was George Burroughs who was ultimately scapegoated? Contemporaries and historians differ over Burroughs' character. Reverend Cotton Mather stated, "glad should I have been, if I had never know the name of this man,"[1] and Magistrate Thomas Hutchinson declared that Burroughs was "a man of bad character, and of a cruel disposition."[2] Two centuries later, Alan Putnam wrote that Burroughs was a "peaceful man and persistent laborer . . . a rare embodiment of the prevailing perception, sentiments, virtues and graces."[3] Later, Robinson claimed Burroughs was a fierce Indian fighter, loyal friend, and dedicated minister, who was murdered by envious men and malicious teenagers.[4]

The few documents that have survived from the period before the Salem witchcraft trails show that George Burroughs had an unblemished life. Despite his respectable reputation, the clergy condemned him as the Devil incarnate, and the magistrates hanged him for diabolism based upon what they believed to be irrefutable evidence: owing a debt, arguing with neighbors, inflicting pain, causing death, possessing superhuman strength, declaring that witches did not exist, resembling the Devil, and leading a coven of witches.[5]

George Burroughs was born in Virginia in 1652 to Rebecca and Nathaniel. As a young man, he was schooled at the Roxbury Latin School by Reverend John Eliot who openly ministered to the Indians. Burroughs, under Eliot's guidance and religious tolerance, also became involved with the American Indians. In 1666, Burroughs moved to Massachusetts to attend Harvard. There, his southern heritage kept him an outsider. Despite this barrier and a small stature, he was hailed as the university's first outstanding athlete; his physical skills were later interpreted as proof of witchcraft.[6]

In 1674, a few years after graduating, he moved back to Roxbury, Massachusetts, and married a woman named Hannah. There Burroughs' tolerant religious nature, which later outraged Cotton Mather, clashed with the intolerant Puritanism of the townspeople.[7] Eventually, religious differences forced Burroughs and his young wife to move to Casco, Maine, a community that accepted both Puritans and non-Puritans.[8] There Burroughs became the town's first minister, receiving two hundred acres of land as part of his pay.[9]

During King Philip's War, the Casco residents were besieged by Indian attacks.[10] George Burroughs wrote to John Hathorne, the Chief Magistrate of Boston, for supplies and soldiers. This first communication ignited a serious of events that would link these men. Burroughs would later marry Hathorne's widowed sister-in-law, and at the witch trials, Hathorne would pronounce Burroughs guilty of diabolism and sentence him to death.[11] Yet at this first contact, Hathorne quickly responded to Burroughs' request for help and sent troops under the command of his younger brother, Captain William Hathorne.

Sadly, in 1678, a smallpox epidemic raged through Casco, killing both Hannah Burroughs and William Hathorne. George and Sarah, now widowed, met, fell in love, and married. John Hathorne protested this marriage, claiming Burroughs was an outsider and a fortune-hunter.[12]

Unfortunately, the Indian attacks continued. Burroughs again wrote to Hathorne for help, but none came. Surrounded by Indians, George Burroughs and his family fled to Salisbury, Massachusetts, where he continued to preach throughout New England to Puritans, non-Puritans, and the Indians.[13] Later, Reverend Cotton Mather, although supported the conversion of the Indians, proclaimed that George Burroughs' ministering to them was proof that he was in league with the Devil.[14]

In 1680, Burroughs heard that the minister of Salem had resigned due to growing conflicts between the villagers and himself over land and with failure to pay his salary. Burroughs offered his services. He was so well-liked that the Salem elect asked him to be their permanent minister, promising to pay him ninety-three pounds and six shillings per year, sixty pounds of goods, and rebuild the old parsonage.[15] John Putnam, a member of the elect, asked the young pastor to live with his family while the house was being rebuilt. Burroughs lived with the Putnam's for none months, but their relationship became strained when the community failed to rebuild the parsonage or pay his wages.[16]

In January 1781, Sarah Burroughs suddenly died and her brother-in-law, John Hathorne, blamed George for her death.[17] Burroughs, raising seven children and unable to control a quarreling congregation, could not pay for his wife's funeral; he borrowed the money from Putnam, an action that further strained their already difficult relationship.[18] By March, the tensions between the two men climaxed and Burroughs resigned, without ever repaying his debt or being paid his wages.[19]

George Burroughs left Salem and returned to Casco, Maine, devoting his life to his children and parishioners. In April, however, the Salem elect sent word that they had agreed to pay him his back wages. Yet when George Burroughs arrived in Salem to collect his money, the embittered John Putnam had him arrested for non-payment of a debt. The warrant read:

> Action of debt of six pounds for two gallons of Canary wine, and cloth, etc., bought of Mr. Gedney on John Putnam's account, for the funeral of Mrs. Burroughs.[20]

On May 2, 1681, George Burroughs stood trial for this debt, although the Salem elect owed him back salary.[21] The magistrate asked, "What goods do you have to pay these debts?"[22] Burroughs replied, "I have no goods to show . . . for we know not yet who is in debt, but there is my body."[23] The Court found George Burroughs guilty of owing a debt and having a wicked character; the magistrate denied Burroughs his wages and banished him from Massachusetts.[24] However, the real issue was not the debt or his character, but the Salem villagers' growing need to blame someone for their escalating problems. Thus, Burroughs, nine years before the Salem outbreak, had been labeled an evil trouble maker.[24]

George Burroughs, banished from Massachusetts, returned to Casco and told his parishioners, "I was glad to get away from those evil men at Salem as I preferred the Indian attacks."[25] However, he became too busy rebuilding the town and tending to the needs of his parishioners to concern himself any further with the problem at Salem. Papers filed in the State House for the District of Maine showed that George Burroughs was caring and generous as he returned most of the land that the Casco residents had originally paid him.[26] Historian Charles Upham wrote that Burroughs was a friend and counselor who ". . . laboring in humility and zeal shared all the pain of his parishioners."[27]

Burroughs, the only Puritan minister in Maine, continued to earn respect by risking his life spreading the Word to those devastated by Indian attacks.

Church records also show that the Indian raids continued, forcing Burroughs and his children to leave and move to Wells, Maine. There, George Burroughs settled and married his third wife, Mary, and fathered another child.[28]

Unfortunately, in May 1691, these villagers also suffered a fierce Indian attack. Again, Burroughs wrote to Magistrate Hathorne for help: "All the people killed and taken . . . must have more assistance."[29] There was no reply. In desperation, he sent another dispatch, this time to the Commander of the Garrison at Boston, Captain Floyd: "The enemy beating upon us . . . [we] make our humble address to your honors for men, with provisions and ammunition."[30] Floyd replied that troops and supplies were on the way. They never came. By September 1691, the town was surrounded and Burroughs pleaded for the last time: "It has pleased God, to let loose the heathens upon us . . . we are brought very low."[31]

A year later, on May 2, 1692, when Field Marshall John Partridge and his troops rode into the war-ravaged town of Wells, the starving and frightened townspeople though he had come with men and provisions.[32] He only carried an arrest warrant that read:

To apprehend the body of Mr. George Burroughs . . . and convey him with all speed to Salem . . . to be examined, he being suspected for a confederacy with the Devil.[33]

Unbeknownst to them, the 'afflicted' girls at Salem had claimed that Burroughs was the 'above' conjuror. An accusation that was not only initiated, but encouraged by the clergy and the Court in their quest to ferret out the root of the evils that were plaguing Salem.

George Burroughs' arrested in Maine for the alleged crimes of witchcraft committed in Salem, and the 'afflicted girls' explosive accusation of diabolism were the turning-points of the Salem witchcraft saga.[34] These two issues clearly show that the hunt, unlike previous New England witch-hunts, had not only spread beyond local boundaries but escalated into a search for blame. George Burroughs, who had survived smallpox epidemics, harsh Maine winters, and brutal Indian attacks, was now the target of a group of malicious girls claiming to be possessed, and a group of pious men claiming to do God's will.[35]

CHAPTER SIX

The Witch-Hunt

Before the 1692 tragedy, several New Englanders had been hanged for witchcraft, but only George Burroughs was executed for diabolism.[1] Although this factor makes the Salem witch-craze unique among the New England witch-hunts, there is another element that singles it out—the Puritan clergy and Salem magistrates' obsession with finding a scapegoat to save the theocracy and bolster their ecclesiastical and political powers. Historian Jeffery Victor claimed the "Salem outbreak was based on a need to find a scapegoat whether in the form of a Devil, at witch, or a neighbor."[2]

The events that transformed the Salem with-craze from a typical hunt for a witch to an obsessive search for the Devil began in May 1692.[3] The Governor of Massachusetts, Sir William Phips, arrived from England with a new charter for Massachusetts Bay, only to find the jails filled with accused witches.[4] On May 8, 1692, he appointed seven special magistrates to the Salem Court of Oyer and Terminer: William Stoughton, Jonathan Corwin, Bartholomew Gedney, John Richards, Nathaniel Saltonstall, Peter Sergeant, John Hathorne, and Samuel Sewall.[5] On that day, Sewall wrote that it was "awful to see how the afflicted persons were agitated by those accused of witchcraft."[6] According to historian Ola Winslow, New England magistrates faced a ghastly task; witchcraft was a crime punishable by death.[7] The existence of witches and the legal grounds to execute them were supported by the Bible, recognized by the Church, and confirmed by the laws of England.

One of the accused witches, George Burroughs, was taken before the Salem magistrates who charged that he had "tortured, afflicted, pined, consumed, wasted, and tormented Mary Walcott, Mercy Lewis, Abagail Williams, Ann Putnam, Elizabeth Hubert, and Susannah Sheldon."[8] George Burroughs replied that he knew nothing of these charges. The magistrates asked him if he had recently partaken in the Lord's Supper, if all his children were baptized, and if his house at Casco was haunted. George Burroughs replied, no, but added that there were toads in his basement.[9] The Court convinced that they had enough evidence, set a trail date.

On August 5, 1692, George Burroughs stood trial again, this time for witchcraft, wizardry, and other 'sundry' acts.[10] After all the testimony was heard, the clergy condemned him as the Devil incarnate and the Court pronounced him guilty of diabolism and sentenced him to death.[11] Also convicted that day, buy only for maleficium and doing harm to a neighbor by witchcraft, were John Proctor and his wife Elizabeth, John Willard, George Jacobs, Sr., and Martha Carrier.[12]

On August 19, the condemned were tied onto a cart and paraded through the streets of Salem to Gallows Hill.[13] On the scaffold, George Burroughs professed his innocence and preceded to recite the Lord's Prayer perfectly; contemporaries believed that a witch or wizard would choke on God's Words and be incapable of such a feat.[14] The crowd, moved by Burroughs' plea of innocence and his flawless recitation, begged for his life. Suddenly, the 'afflicted' shouted that a 'black man' had dictated the Lord's Prayer to him.[15] Reverend Cotton Mather, convinced that George Burroughs was the Devil incarnate, rode his horse into the crowd and quoted from 2 Corinthians 11:14: "For Satan himself is transformed into an angel of light." [16]Mather ordered Burroughs hanged. After his death, George Burroughs body was cut down, dragged to a shallow hole, stripped and dressed in old trousers, and buried next to Martha Carrier "so fast that one of his hands and his chin and a foot was left uncovered."[17]

However, the execution of George Burroughs had sowed seeds of doubt; villagers began questioning how a Puritan minister could be the Devil when a man of the cloth could not be corrupted, and how a witch could recite the Lord's Prayer perfectly.[18] The authorities, to quell the growing suspicions, continued the hunt: Magistrate Stoughton signed six more death warrants, the Reverend Cotton Mather declared that "the jury brought him [George Burroughs] in guilty," [19]Increase Mather openly stated that "had I been one of the Judges, I could not have acquitted him," and Magistrate Sewall reassured the townspeople that "five witches were hanged on Gallows Hill . . . they all died by a Righteous Sentence."[20]

CHAPTER SEVEN

What say the Afflicted?

Some historians theorize that the New England clergy and Salem magistrates not only initiated, but spread the Salem witch-craze. Silverman argues that the clergy influenced the accusers' testimonies and swayed the magistrates' verdicts.[1] Hansen contends that the Salem witch-craze was flamed by the authorities' obsession with finding guilt.[2] Historian Thomas Schoeneman maintains that witchcraft was brought into the Courts by zealous ministers,[3] while Robinson adds that it was specifically the Reverend Cotton Mather who laid the ground work for the Salem witchcraft trials.[4]

In 1692, New England's religious and the political structures were in turmoil. The clergy and magistrates were desperate to save a faltering theocracy; villagers were rejecting the covenant, spurning the godly way of life, and moving to the frontier for more land.[5] In an attempt to regain control, judges imposed the death penalty for such minor offenses as divination and fortune-telling, and ministers reminded every villager of his or her Christian duty to seek out and destroy evil.[6] Reverend Lawson admonished his congregation that Satan had to be stopped, while Pastor Parris entitled a 1692 sermon: "There are devils as well as saints in Christ's church—One of you is a devil."[7] The Reverend Cotton Mather also prophesied that "Satan would arrest the country out of their hands."[8]

The authorities proclaimed that failure to obey the secular laws and Puritan tenets would result in God allowing the Devil and his witches to live among them.[9] Calef, horrified by these messages, warned that "threatened the destruction of this country."[10] Still, the frightened villagers continued to suspect evil forces behind every natural disaster, failing crops, unexplained illness, sudden death, Indian attack, and anyone who went against the Puritan standards. With all eyes looking for evil, it should not be surprising that a witch-hunt would erupt.

Witch-hunts typically occur in times of social, political, and religious upheavals.[11] Robinson claims that hunts based upon charges of maleficium were commonplace, ignited by villagers, and never extended beyond local boundaries.[12] On the other hand, hunts centered upon diabolism were rare, often spread beyond local boundaries, and sought a scapegoat. In addition, hunts for a scapegoat could not develop unless there was sufficient ecclesiastical and judicial authority to arrest, prosecute, imprison, and enforce the death penalty.[13]

The Salem outbreak was such a hunt. Although it began when a group of teenage girls claimed to be possessed by witches, their accusations provided the clergy and magistrates with the opportunity to form an alliance that issued arrest warrants, initiated the trials, launched a hunt for a scapegoat, and carried out executions to save a deteriorating theocracy. For the ministers, ferreting out the Devil and his witches would prove there was an evil conspiracy to destroy New England, frightening the dissenters back into the fold.[14] For the magistrates, executing the enemies of society, the Devil and his witches, would restore their waning power. For both groups, the Salem Meeting house became the battleground between God's elect and the Devil's legions.[15]

Motivated by the possibility of ecclesiastical, political, and personal gains, the clergy and the Court organized a methodically directed the witch trials by coercing witnesses and allowing fraudulent testimony.[16] As a result, a simple hunt for a witch was transformed into an obsession with finding the Devil.

The most vocal and powerful member of this alliance, however, was not the ruthless William Stoughton nor the vengeful John Hathorne, but the relentless and over zealous Reverend Cotton Mather.[17] Before the 1692 witch-craze, Cotton Mather had been concerned with the evil forces of the invisible world that were causing excessive drunkenness and prostitution in New England.[18] In 1698, however, he met Martha Goodwin, a young girl who claimed to be possessed by a servant, Goody Glover. When the Court found Goody Glover guilty of witch-craft, Mather told his congregation that God had permitted this case to occur so that all the New England witches would be exposed.[19] Mather proclaimed that he ad resolved "never to use just one grain of patience with any man that shall go to impose upon me a denial of the Devil, or of witches."[20] The Goodwin case had proved to Reverend Mather that not only were there invisible evil spirits, but something more dreadful and tangible, witches.[21] As a result, the Goodwin case served as the catalyst for Reverend Mather's fixation with finding the Devil and his league of witches at Salem.

At the 1692 outbreak, the ministers and judges became obsessed with finding the Devil. Given their patriarchal beliefs that God's Kingdom was built on a powerful male hierarchy, they also believed then so must be the Devil's Dominion.[22] Subsequently, the evils that were tormenting Salem could only be the work of the mighty Devil. Yet only old and poor female witches accused of maleficium had been brought before the Court.[23] Therefore, in order to substantiate their belief in the existence of dual male-dominated supernatural spheres, a search for a potent and prominent male witch ensued.

On August 5, 1692, however, their quest ended when Reverend George Burroughs was delivered in shackles to the Salem Meeting house.[24] The authorities instantly seized the opportunity and focused their attention on him; who better a target as a powerful Devil leading a coven of weak females than a Puritan minister, in which the current establishment, at one time, owed him back wages. George Burroughs witch-craft conviction would certainly leave a more lasting impact on the villagers than that of John Willard, an insignificant innkeeper; Samuel Wardell, a fortune-teller; George Jacobs Sr., an old man; John Proctor, a small land owner; or Wilmot Reed, a vagrant.[25]

George Burroughs' conviction for witch-craft would also serve as a warning to the dissenters that the Devil could corrupt anyone, even a man of the cloth. More importantly, his execution for diabolism would prove that the clergy and magistrates were more powerful than the Devil, forcing the villagers to recognize that returning to the Church was their only means of salvation.[26]

How George Burroughs initially became ensnared in the Salem witch mania, whether by the 'afflicted,' clergy, or magistrates continue to remain a mystery. Trial transcripts, however, clearly show that once he was arrested and charged with witch-craft, he became the sole focus of the Salem witch-craft trials.[27]

The first to testify against George Burroughs were the 'afflicted.' It was their testimony of subjective and anecdotal evidence that was paramount for the authorities search for the Devil, the quintessential rebel against God. The magistrates and clergy declared that those that stood before and accused the Devil incarnate were protected by God's law.[28] This God's law did not allow accusers to lie. Therefore, if one was accused of being a witch, the accusation *must* be true.[29]

Evidence from 1692 witch-craft trail transcripts shows that the clergy and magistrates not only encouraged the 'afflicted' to testify in the name of God, but coerced the accused to confess to making a pact with the Devil.[30] Bailey claims that the trials were characterized by the authorities' implanting and often forcing religious guilt.[31] At her witch-craft trial, Martha Tyler proclaimed her innocence. Reverend John Emerson insisted she was guilty of being a witch; he not only claimed that he saw the Devil standing beside her, but that God's law cannot and will not allow her accusers to lie; and therefore it is true that she is a witch.[32] Yet, when Martha refused to confess, Reverend Emerson threatened, "I leave you undone, body and soul, forever."[33] In fear of her soul, Martha Tyler confessed to witch-craft and was condemned to death.[34]

Another accused witch, Mercy Wardell, also refused to confess. Magistrate John Higginson told her that she would never marry, as no man would wed a convicted witch.[35] However, if she confessed and recanted, she would be vindicated of all charges. Despondent over the prospect of being a spinster, Mercy Wardell confessed to witch-craft, claiming she would not live alone.[36]

Sarah Wilson, also jailed for refusing to confess to witch-craft, was visited by Increase Mather. In order to obtain a confession, he tried to convince her that being possessed was not her fault; and women were weaker and had feeble minds which were that much more susceptible to being possessed.[37] He went on by telling her that the Devil could possess someone without his or her knowledge, especially women. Sarah remained steadfast, claiming that a confession would be a lie and an offense to God. Increase Mather then asked had she ever made a pact with the Devil and how she knew she was not a witch. She replied that she had never made a pact with the Devil, but was "in the dark as being a witch . . . seeing the afflicted in pain [makes me] believe that [my] spirit must be possessed by the evil eye."[38] Thus, she was convinced that she could be a witch and confessed.

At Salem, although obtaining a confession was the primary goal, the clergy and magistrates relied on the 'afflicted' girls' testimony for saving souls and guilty verdicts than on extracting confessions. Magistrates Stoughton and Hathorne believed every word of the girls' testimony, while Reverend Cotton Mather provided 'expert' support for their witch-craft claims and Samuel Parris took their depositions and recorded the trial testimony.[39]

The first of the Salem witches brought to trial was Bridget Bishop, a tavern owner and a woman of ill-repute. The 'afflicted' claimed to have been bewitched by Bishop. Reverend John Hale, a Puritan minister and a well known New England witch-hunter, asked the 'afflicted' girls did she use 'poppet's' and where did she keep them.[40] The 'afflicted' replied that she kept them in her basement. Hale went to the tavern and demanded to search her basement. Finding a 'poppet,' he reported to the Court that the girl's were telling the truth. Bridget Bishop was convicted of being a witch and running a place of iniquity and was in consort with the Devil.[41]

The 'afflicted' then reported to Reverend Parris that Susanna Martin was a witch. Parris took their depositions and testified that to the validity of the claims. On the witness-stand, the 'afflicted' swore that a black man was whispering in Martin's ear. Susanna laughed.[42] The girls screamed. The clergy leaped to the 'afflicted' defense and tried to shield the girls from Martin's 'evil eye' with their bodies, but the 'afflicted' continued to scream.⁴³ The judges ordered Martin to stop hurting them. Martin laughed louder, claiming that the authorities were as mad as the so called 'afflicted.' ⁴⁴ The 'afflicted' continued to scream and then began convulsing. The judges found Susanna Martin guilty and she was immediately hanged.⁴⁵

The 'afflicted' then charged that Sarah Good had also possessed them. The magistrates asked if she knew the Devil. Sarah answered, no. The magistrates asked her why then were these innocent children being hurt. She replied, I do not know. Hathorne then ordered the 'afflicted' to point their finger at Sarah Good, declaring her a witch.⁴⁶ They did. Sarah shouted, "Now see what you have done. I have not tormented them, thus you torment the children."⁴⁷

Yet in 1692, participants and critics of the witch-craft trials began to see the fraudulent accusations and the unholy dependence between the authorities and the 'afflicted.' Calef reported that at the trail of Martha Carrier, the Salem girls claimed that a black man was hovering around her.⁴⁸ Martha replied that "[she] saw no black man, but only your own presence your honor."⁴⁹ She was found guilty of witch-craft and hanged. Reverend Thomas Brattle stated, "The witches were apprehended purely on the complaints of the afflicted . . . whoever they accused, the Court found the guilty."⁵⁰ Levin claimed that the 'afflicted' owned the Justices by providing them with the names of the guilty, and tricking the ministers of God that they were being instructed by the Devil.⁵¹ Reverend John Hale, seeing the deception, refused to arrest another Salem witch on the testimony of the 'afflicted.' He wrote that the authorities were so eager to have the girls testify that "there can be no question that . . . [they] held the most credulous views as to the worth of the testimony of the afflicted."⁵²

However, the alliance between the clergy and Court and their dependence upon the testimony of the 'afflicted' set the stage for the Salem witch-hunt to escalate into a search for the leader of these witches. Thus, when George Burroughs was charged with the crime of witch-craft and brought before the Court, he became the target of this unholy alliance. Encouraged by the authorities, the 'afflicted' told outlandish tales, swearing they had seen and been hurt by Burroughs' specter, a sign of witch-craft.⁵³ Susannah Sheldon said Burroughs' specter told her that he had murdered his wives,⁵⁴ while Mary Warren claimed his specter had offered her wine that was really blood.⁵⁵ Mercy Lewis, who had lived with the Burroughs' family after her parents were killed in an Indian attack, stated, "I saw the apparition of George Burroughs . . . [He said] he could raise the Devil."⁵⁶ Finally, Abigail Hobbs claimed she had hurt Salem villagers with 'poppets.' The magistrates asked, "Who brought those poppets to you?"⁵⁷ She answered, "The specter of Mr. Burroughs,"⁵⁸ The magistrates asked her, "How did you know Mr. Burroughs was a witch?" She replied, 'Because he told me so."⁵⁹

Hearing this testimony, the authorities concentrated on George Burroughs; he was being accused of more heinous crimes than previous accused witches. According to Demos, the Salem witch-craze was ignited by the hostilities of some young girls against authority figures.[60] Thus, in the clergy and Court's compulsion to find the Devil, they prompted the 'afflicted' to direct their allegations from old men and poor women to this prominent member of the community. The leader of the 'afflicted,' Ann Putman, provided them with such evidence when she claimed that Burroughs had forced her to sign the Devil's book, a sign of witch-craft.[61]

Nine years earlier, when Ann Putnam was only three years old, Burroughs had lived with the Putnam family. He become the center of attention when a Salem magistrate convicted him of owing Ann's father, John Putnam, a debt, and banished him from Massachusetts for having a wicked character. At the Salem witch-craft trials, Ann testified that, "he tortured me and urged me to write in his book, which I refused. Then he told me his name was George Burroughs and he was an 'above' witch."[62] Thus, it is a fair assumption that Ann Putnam, remembering Burroughs from her childhood and being supported by the clergy and Court, chose him as the Devil.

The next to testify were Burroughs' neighbors from Casco, Maine and residents of Salem. The Casco villagers, weary from years of attacks by Indians, the "Devil's agents," were easily convinced by the authorities to testify against Burroughs. The Salem residents, frustrated from years of local conflicts over land, were also easily manipulated into venting their repressed anger with slanderous witch-craft accusations against Burroughs.[63] These accusers claimed that George Burroughs had super-human strength, another sign of witch-craft. As a student, Burroughs had been an outstanding athlete. As an adult, he had worded side-by-side with his parishioners; now these once applauded qualities were seen as the work of the Devil. Samuel Webber stated that "[Burroughs] put his finger into a bung barrel of molasses and lifted it up;"[64] Captain Simon Willard swore that "Mr. Burroughs [could] hold out his gun with one hand;"[65] and William Wormall declared that Burroughs could lift a barrel of glass all by himself." [66]Captain Daniel King, a close friend of Burroughs and fellow Indian fighter, attested that "Burroughs was a child of God . . . and that God would clear up his innocence."[67] The Court of Oyer and Terminer dismissed Captain King's statement as worthless, concluding that as Burroughs was such a small man, he could have only done these physical feats with the help of the Devil."[68]

As the trial continued, the Court reassured the towns people that all the witches would be destroyed and the Devil expelled from the land. The magistrates, hoping to find more physical evidence against Burroughs, ordered seven jurors to search his small, dark body for witches' treats. None were found.[69] The Reverend Cotton Mather pointed out to the Court that while witches could conceal marks, the Bible clearly stated that the Devil always exhibited himself as a small black man.[70] As if rehearsed, the 'afflicted' screamed and fell to the floor in fits when Mather made this declaration. Abagail Williams cried out that she had seen a little black minister, who claimed he lived in Casco Bay and had killed his wives.[71] Elizabeth Hubbard shouted that a small, black wizard had appeared to her, saying his name was Burroughs.[72] Historian Jeffery Victor claimed that this testimony rendered Burroughs and the Devil synonymous.[73]

Yet the evidence that convicted the clergy and magistrates they had captured the Devil, came from the testimonies of eight confessed Andover witches.[74] The Andover witch-craze began when two of Salem's 'afflicted,' Ann Putnam and Abagail Williams, went to see the constable's sick wife; they declared that she was not sick but bewitched. As a result, a witch-hunt exploded and over fifty Andover residents confessed that ". . . they [had] ridden through the air on poles . . . were baptized by the Devil . . . [and] signed his Book."[75] Eight of the confessed testified that George Burroughs was their leader and had given them a mission to destroy the Church of God, and to set up Satan's Kingdom at Salem."[76]

This explosive testimony made George Burroughs a scapegoat not only for the authorities and the 'afflicted,' but also for the Andover witches. Pressured by family members and persuaded by the ministers to confess to witch-craft, the witches were also promised freedom from the gallows by the Andover Court if they named the Devil, the Andover accused complied.[77] Ann Foster, the first of the accused Andover witches to confess, declared she had ridden on a stick to a witches' Sabbath.[78] There, she and other witches had inflicted pain on the Salem residents by squeezing 'poppets.'[79] The Andover Court found her guilty, but set her free when she said Burroughs was the Devil.[80] The news quickly spread. One by one, seven more confessed Andover witches claimed that Burroughs, a man whom they had never met, was their leader; all were released.[81]

It is not a mystery that these deluded witches chose to name Burroughs in order to escape the hangman's noose, as Ann Putnam and Abagail Williams had originally told them that he was the 'above' conjuror.[82]

The confessed Andover witches were brought to the Salem Meeting house. Upon hearing the testimony, the Court declared that the confessions were absolute proof of George Burroughs' guilt. The 'afflicted' fell writhing to the floor. The Court ask Burroughs what he thought. Appearing confused, he replied ". . . it is amazing."[83] but he "understood nothing of it."[84] Magistrate Stoughton then asked him who was hurting these people. He answered, "I suppose it [is] the Devil."[85]

Within a few minutes, however, George Burroughs regained his composure and took the witness stand. He stated that he had proof of his innocence.

Taking a piece of paper from his coat pocket, he read it to the Court: "There neither are, nor ever were witches, that having made a compact with the Devil, can send a Devil to torment other people at a distance."[86] He declared that witches did not exist; moreover, he insisted that he could not be the Devil as Satan could only hurt those who were near him. Therefore, he had to be innocent of all charges given that he lived in Maine and the 'afflicted' lived in Massachusetts.[87] The judges conferred with Reverend Cotton Mather, who proclaimed that George Burroughs had not given proof of his innocence, but had read a passage from Thomas Ady's blasphemous book, *A Candle in the Dark*, that denounced the existence of witches and witch-craft.[88] Mather advised the Court that George Burroughs' knowledge of and access to this evil work and along with being found guilt of having a wicked character was proof that he was in league with the Devil.[89] The magistrates agreed. Historian John Sibley claimed that Cotton Mather's "expert" advice led the Court to dismiss Burroughs' evidence of innocence and allow only testimony that would ensure a guilty verdict.[90]

With the testimony over and Reverend Burroughs securely shackled to a bench in the Salem Meeting house, the Court deliberated. Cotton Mather reminded the judges that Burroughs was the 'Master Conspirator,' as thirty witnesses had identified him as a witch.[91] Swayed by this statement, the Court found George Burroughs guilty of witch-craft and sentenced him to death for diabolism. The authorities, thereby, had succeeded in their obsessive quest to ferret out and expose the Devil. Magistrate Hathorne, still blaming Burroughs for the death of his younger brother and sister-in-law, asked for the honor of pronouncing the death sentence.[92] The Court granted his request. However, it was Cotton Mather's hatred of Burroughs' liberal Puritan standards and religious tolerances that outweighed Hathorne's revenge, the girls' maliciousness, the villagers' slander, and the Andover witches' fear of the gallows.[93]

On August 19, 1692, the Reverend George Burroughs was hanged for being the Devil incarnate. The clergy and magistrates heralded each other as God's champions. Magistrate Stoughton wrote to Cotton Mather: "Thankfulness to you . . . the spirit of the Lord has thus enabled you to lift up a standard against the infernal enemy."[94] Mather wrote back to the Court that "Almighty God [had] graciously enclined their Majesties to favour us by expelling the Devil from the land."[95] Yet with Burroughs' death, the villagers did not hail these men as God's champions, but questioned the validity of the witches trials.

Reverend George Burroughs was not only an unfortunate victim of the Salem witch-hunt, but its scapegoat; the ideal person to blame for personal misfortunes, local grievances, social and religious upheavals, and a disintegrating theocracy.[96] Burroughs, the only accused New England witch to be accused and executed for being the Devil incarnate, fulfilled all the requirements. Court records showed he had been banished from Massachusetts for arguing with a member of the Salem Elect and owing a debt; he admitted that he had been too busy fighting Indians to attend Church regularly, partake of the last supper, or baptize his children; he had that there were toads in his house, had access to a blasphemous book, and did not believe in witches; and, he had been accused of tormenting the 'afflicted,' having superhuman strength, resembling the Devil, and being the leader of a witches' coven. The mounting evidence against Burroughs provided the clergy and magistrates with the proof they needed to find him guilty of witch-craft and execute him for diabolism; thus, validating the witch trials and the executions. Calef, however, summed up best the George Burroughs' tragedy asserting that these Puritan leaders had allowed "an innocent man to be hanged solely on an obsession."[97]

CHAPTER EIGHT

Closing of the Witch-Hunt

On September 29, 1692, the last of the convicted witches were hanged.[1] The Salem witch-craft trails had ended. Yet Magistrate Stoughton continued to hear testimony against George Burroughs, obsessed with proving that Satan had been hanged.[2] Reverend Parris refused to stop preaching fiery witch-craft sermons and was banished.[3] Reverend Cotton Mather, until his death, proclaimed that the Devil and "real" witches had been executed.[4]

However, most of the towns people admitted that innocent people had been hanged. Magistrate Sewall publically asked for forgiveness.[5] The Andover Court released all the convicted witches from jail, condemning the trials and blaming the accusers of being 'distempered persons.'[6] Most of the 'afflicted' girls moved away. Ann Putnam, however, remained in Salem and asked for forgiveness, maintaining she had been deluded by Satan.[7] Many witnesses against George Burroughs asked for mercy, claiming they had been tricked. Calef continued his criticisms declaring, ". . . although the magistrates hanged George Burroughs by the neck, it was Cotton Mather who orchestrated the execution."[8]

The family of George Burroughs, however did not recover as well. In 1693, Burroughs widow, Mary, remarried, leaving seven children to support themselves. The three oldest children, Rebecca, Hannah, and Elizabeth, were forced into early marriage, while the four younger children, George Jr., Charles, Jeremiah, and Josiah, were orphaned. George Jr. wrote to the Court for help: "Our father's small estate was lost and we scattered."[9] The Court made John Ruck, the maternal grandfather, the children's guardian for which he received two hundred dollars a year. Unfortunately, Ruck profited. Again, George Jr. petitioned the Court:

Although our father was executed, he was innocent and we earnestly pray that the attainder may be taken off, and the fifty pounds may be restored.[10]

The children of George Burroughs never received any articles or monies from their father's estate.

In 1711, the guilty conviction of George Burroughs was reversed.[11] The children petitioned again for restitution. In 1713, each child was given six pounds for the wrongful murder of their father; the balance after the executioner's fee was paid.[12] In 1996, three hundred of his descendants, held their annual convention of the Newman Society at Gallows Hill, Salem, Massachusetts, to honor the man . . . George Burroughs.

CHAPTER ONE REFERENCES

1. Boyer, P. (1976). *Salem possessed: The social origins of witchcraft.* Cambridge, MA: Harvard University Press.

2. Jaques, E. (1954). Social systems as defense against persecutory and depressive anxiety. In M. Klein, P. Heimann & R.E. Money-Kyrle (Eds.), *New directions in psycho-analysis* (pp. 478—498). New York: Basic Books.

3. Klein, M. (1958). One the development of mental functioning. *International Journal of Psychoanalysis, 39,* 84-90.

4. Menzies-Lyth, I. (1988). *Containing anxiety in institutions: Selected essays.* London: Free Association Books.

5. Segal, H. (1973). *Introduction to the work of Melanie Klein.* New York: Basic Books

6. Miller, A. (1990). *For your own good: Hidden cruelty in childrearing and the roots of violence.* (Hildegard and Hunter, Trans.). New York: Noonday Press.

7. Roach, M. (2004). *The Salem witch trials: A day-by-day chronicle of a community under siege.* Lanham, MD: Taylor Trade Publishing.

8. Klein, M. (1946). Notes on some schizoid mechanisms. *International Journal of Psychoanalysis, 27,* 99-110.

9. Klein, M. (1958). One the development of mental functioning. *International Journal of Psychoanalysis, 39,* 84-90.

10. Menzies-Lyth, I. (1960). A case in the functioning of social systems as a defense against anxiety: A report on a study of nursing service of a general hospital. *Human Relations, 13*, 95-121.

11. Menzies-Lyth, I. (1988). *Containing anxiety in institutions: Selected essays.* London: Free Association Books.

12. Reed, I. (2007). Why Salem made sense: Culture, gender, and the Puritan persecution of witchcraft. *Cultural Sociology 1*(2): 209-234.

13. Bion, W.R. (1954). Group dynamics: A re-view. In M. Klein, P. Heimann & R.E. Money-Kyrle (Eds.), *New directions in psycho-analysis* (pp. 440-477). New York: Basic Books.

14. Levin, D. (1960). *What happened in Salem?* New York: Harcourt, Brace and Company.

15. Bion, W.R. (1954). Group dynamics: A re-view. In M. Klein, P. Heimann & R.E. Money-Kyrle (Eds.), *New directions in psycho-analysis* (pp. 440-477). New York: Basic Books.

16. Bion, W.R. (1954). Group dynamics: A re-view. In M. Klein, P. Heimann & R.E. Money-Kyrle (Eds.), *New directions in psycho-analysis* (pp. 440-477). New York: Basic Books.

17. Levin, D. (1960). *What happened in Salem?* New York: Harcourt, Brace and Company.

18. Jaques, E. (1954). Social systems as defense against persecutory and depressive anxiety. In M. Klein, P. Heimann & R.E. Money-Kyrle (Eds.), *New directions in psycho-analysis* (pp. 478—498). New York: Basic Books.

19. Jaques, E. (1954). Social systems as defense against persecutory and depressive anxiety. In M. Klein, P. Heimann & R.E. Money-Kyrle (Eds.), *New directions in psycho-analysis* (pp. 478—498). New York: Basic Books.

20. Klein, M. (1946). Notes on some schizoid mechanisms. *International Journal of Psychoanalysis, 27*, 99-110.

21. Klein, M. (1958). One the development of mental functioning. *International Journal of Psychoanalysis*, *39*, 84-90.

22. Bion, W.R. (1954). Group dynamics: A re-view. In M. Klein, P. Heimann & R.E. Money-Kyrle (Eds.), *New directions in psycho-analysis* (pp. 440-477). New York: Basic Books.

23. Bion, W.R. (1954). Group dynamics: A re-view. In M. Klein, P. Heimann & R.E. Money-Kyrle (Eds.), *New directions in psycho-analysis* (pp. 440-477). New York: Basic Books.

24. Dreyfus, H. L., & Rabinow, P. (1983). *Michel Foucault, beyond structuralism and hermeneutics*. Chicago, University of Chicago Press.

25. Kane, A. (1991). "Cultural Analysis in Historical Sociology." *Sociological Theory* 9(1): 53-69.

26. Bion, W.R. (1954). Group dynamics: A re-view. In M. Klein, P. Heimann & R.E. Money-Kyrle (Eds.), *New directions in psycho-analysis* (pp. 440-477). New York: Basic Books.

27. Klein, M. (1958). One the development of mental functioning. *International Journal of Psychoanalysis*, *39*, 84-90.

28. Bion, W.R. (1954). Group dynamics: A re-view. In M. Klein, P. Heimann & R.E. Money-Kyrle (Eds.), *New directions in psycho-analysis* (pp. 440-477). New York: Basic Books.

29. Jaques, E. (1954). Social systems as defense against persecutory and depressive anxiety. In M. Klein, P. Heimann & R.E. Money-Kyrle (Eds.), *New directions in psycho-analysis* (pp. 478—498). New York: Basic Books.

30. Jaques, E. (1954). Social systems as defense against persecutory and depressive anxiety. In M. Klein, P. Heimann & R.E. Money-Kyrle (Eds.), *New directions in psycho-analysis* (pp. 478—498). New York: Basic Books.

31. Jaques, E. (1954). Social systems as defense against persecutory and depressive anxiety. In M. Klein, P. Heimann & R.E. Money-Kyrle

(Eds.), *New directions in psycho-analysis* (pp. 478—498). New York: Basic Books.

32. Hazell, C. (2005). *Imaginary Groups*. Bloomington, Indiana: Authorhouse.

33. Klein, M. (1946). Notes on some schizoid mechanisms. *International Journal of Psychoanalysis*, 27, 99-110.

34. Klein, M. (1958). One the development of mental functioning. *International Journal of Psychoanalysis*, 39, 84-90.

35. Bion, W.R. (1954). Group dynamics: A re-view. In M. Klein, P. Heimann & R.E. Money-Kyrle (Eds.), *New directions in psycho-analysis* (pp. 440-477). New York: Basic Books.

36. Bion, W.R. (1954). Group dynamics: A re-view. In M. Klein, P. Heimann & R.E. Money-Kyrle (Eds.), *New directions in psycho-analysis* (pp. 440-477). New York: Basic Books.

37. Dreyfus, H. L., & Rabinow, P. (1983). *Michel Foucault, beyond structuralism and hermeneutics*. Chicago, University of Chicago Press.

38. Kane, A. (1991). "Cultural Analysis in Historical Sociology." *Sociological Theory* 9(1): 53-69.

39. Levin, D. (1960). *What happened in Salem?* New York: Harcourt, Brace and Company.

40. Bion, W.R. (1954). Group dynamics: A re-view. In M. Klein, P. Heimann & R.E. Money-Kyrle (Eds.), *New directions in psycho-analysis* (pp. 440-477). New York: Basic Books.

41. Boyer, P. (1976). *Salem possessed: The social origins of witchcraft*. Cambridge, MA: Harvard University Press.

42. Jaques, E. (1954). Social systems as defense against persecutory and depressive anxiety. In M. Klein, P. Heimann & R.E. Money-Kyrle (Eds.), *New directions in psycho-analysis* (pp. 478—498). New York: Basic Books.

43. Klein, M. (1958). One the development of mental functioning. *International Journal of Psychoanalysis*, *39*, 84-90.

44. Menzies-Lyth, I. (1988). *Containing anxiety in institutions: Selected essays*. London: Free Association Books.

45. Segal, H. (1973). *Introduction to the work of Melanie Klein*. New York: Basic Books

46. Miller, A. (1990). *For your own good: Hidden cruelty in childrearing and the roots of violence*. (Hildegard and Hunter, Trans.). New York: Noonday Press.

47. Roach, M. (2004). *The Salem witch trials: A day-by-day chronicle of a community under siege*. Lanham, MD: Taylor Trade Publishing.

48. Klein, M. (1946). Notes on some schizoid mechanisms. *International Journal of Psychoanalysis*, *27*, 99-110.

49. Klein, M. (1958). One the development of mental functioning. *International Journal of Psychoanalysis*, *39*, 84-90.

50. Menzies-Lyth, I. (1960). A case in the functioning of social systems as a defense against anxiety: A report on a study of nursing service of a general hospital. *Human Relations*, *13*, 95-121.

51. Boyer, P. (1976). *Salem possessed: The social origins of witchcraft*. Cambridge, MA: Harvard University Press.

52. Jaques, E. (1954). Social systems as defense against persecutory and depressive anxiety. In M. Klein, P. Heimann & R.E. Money-Kyrle (Eds.), *New directions in psycho-analysis* (pp. 478—498). New York: Basic Books.

53. Klein, M. (1958). One the development of mental functioning. *International Journal of Psychoanalysis*, *39*, 84-90.

54. Menzies-Lyth, I. (1988). *Containing anxiety in institutions: Selected essays*. London: Free Association Books.

55. Segal, H. (1973). *Introduction to the work of Melanie Klein*. New York: Basic Books

56. Miller, A. (1990). *For your own good: Hidden cruelty in childrearing and the roots of violence.* (Hildegard and Hunter, Trans.). New York: Noonday Press.

57. Roach, M. (2004). *The Salem witch trials: A day-by-day chronicle of a community under siege.* Lanham, MD: Taylor Trade Publishing.

58. Klein, M. (1946). Notes on some schizoid mechanisms. *International Journal of Psychoanalysis, 27*, 99-110.

59. Klein, M. (1958). One the development of mental functioning. *International Journal of Psychoanalysis, 39*, 84-90.

60. Menzies-Lyth, I. (1960). A case in the functioning of social systems as a defense against anxiety: A report on a study of nursing service of a general hospital. *Human Relations, 13*, 95-121.

61. Klein, M. (1946). Notes on some schizoid mechanisms. *International Journal of Psychoanalysis, 27*, 99-110.

62. Klein, M. (1958). One the development of mental functioning. *International Journal of Psychoanalysis, 39*, 84-90.

63. Bion, W.R. (1954). Group dynamics: A re-view. In M. Klein, P. Heimann & R.E. Money-Kyrle (Eds.), *New directions in psycho-analysis* (pp. 440-477). New York: Basic Books.

64. Bion, W.R. (1954). Group dynamics: A re-view. In M. Klein, P. Heimann & R.E. Money-Kyrle (Eds.), *New directions in psycho-analysis* (pp. 440-477). New York: Basic Books.

65. Dreyfus, H. L., P. Rabinow, et al. (1983). *Michel Foucault, beyond structuralism and hermeneutics.* Chicago, University of Chicago Press.

66. Kane, A. (1991). "Cultural Analysis in Historical Sociology." *Sociological Theory 9*(1): 53-69.

67. Klein, M. (1958). One the development of mental functioning. *International Journal of Psychoanalysis, 39*, 84-90.

68. Menzies-Lyth, I. (1960). A case in the functioning of social systems as a defense against anxiety: A report on a study of nursing service of a general hospital. *Human Relations, 13*, 95-121.

69. Boyer, P. (1976). *Salem possessed: The social origins of witchcraft.* Cambridge, MA: Harvard University Press.

70. Jaques, E. (1954). Social systems as defense against persecutory and depressive anxiety. In M. Klein, P. Heimann & R.E. Money-Kyrle (Eds.), *New directions in psycho-analysis* (pp. 478—498). New York: Basic Books.

71. Klein, M. (1958). One the development of mental functioning. *International Journal of Psychoanalysis, 39*, 84-90.

72. Menzies-Lyth, I. (1988). *Containing anxiety in institutions: Selected essays.* London: Free Association Books.

73. Segal, H. (1973). *Introduction to the work of Melanie Klein.* New York: Basic Books

74. Miller, A. (1990). *For your own good: Hidden cruelty in childrearing and the roots of violence.* (Hildegard and Hunter, Trans.). New York: Noonday Press.

75. Roach, M. (2004). *The Salem witch trials: A day-by-day chronicle of a community under siege.* Lanham, MD: Taylor Trade Publishing.

76. Klein, M. (1946). Notes on some schizoid mechanisms. *International Journal of Psychoanalysis, 27*, 99-110.

77. Klein, M. (1958). One the development of mental functioning. *International Journal of Psychoanalysis, 39*, 84-90.

CHAPTER TWO REFERENCES

1. Allport, G. (1948). *ABC's of scapegoating*. Chicago: Roosevelt College.

2. Campbell, J. (2004). *Pathways to bliss: Mythology and personal transformation*. Novato, CA: New World Library.

3. Girard, R. (1987). Generative scapegoating. In Hamerton & Kelly (Eds.), *Violent origins: Ritual killing and cultural formation*. (pp. 73-145). Stanford, CA: Stanford University Press.

4. Perera, S. B. (1986). *The scapegoat complex: Toward a mythology of shadow and guilt*. Toronto: Inner City Books.

5. Whitmont, E. C. (1991). The evolution of the shadow. In C. Zweig & J Abrams (Eds.), *Meeting the shadow: The hidden power of the dark side of human nature* (pp. 12-19). New York: Tarcher/Putnam.

6. Wilcox, C. W. (2009). *Scapegoat: Targeted for blame*. Denver, CO: Outskirt Press.

7. Perera, S. B. (1986). *The scapegoat complex: Toward a mythology of shadow and guilt*. Toronto: Inner City Books.

8. Wilcox, C. W. (2009). *Scapegoat: Targeted for blame*. Denver, CO: Outskirt Press.

CHAPTER THREE REFERENCES

1. Burr, G. L. (1975). *Narratives of the witchcraft cases, 1648-1706.* New York, NY: Scribner.

2. Marshall, R. (1995). *Witchcraft: The history and mythology.* New York, NY: Random House.

3. Levin, D. (1960). *What happened in Salem? Documents pertaining to the 17th Century witchcraft trials.* New York, NY: Harbrace.

4. Karlsen, C. (1987). *The devil in the shape of a woman: Witchcraft in colonial New England.* New York: Norton.

5. Putnam, A. (1881). *Witchcraft of New England explained by modern spiritualism.* Boston, MA: Colby & Rich.

6. Schoeneman, T. (1975). The witchhunt as a cultural change phenomena. *Ethos, 3*(4), 528-536.

7. Starkey, M. L. (1949). *The devil in Massachusetts: A modern inquiry into the Salem witch trials.* New York, NY: Knopf.

8. Levin, D. (1960). *What happened in Salem? Documents pertaining to the 17th Century witchcraft trials.* New York, NY: Harbrace.

9. Victor, J. (1992). The search for scapegoat deviants. *The Humanist, 52,* 10-13.

CHAPTER FOUR REFERENCES

1. Burr, G. L. (1975). *Narratives of the witchcraft cases, 1648-1706.* New York, NY: Scribner.

2. Marshall, R. (1995). *Witchcraft: The history and mythology.* New York, NY: Random House.

3. Levin, D. (1960). *What happened in Salem? Documents pertaining to the 17th Century witchcraft trials.* New York, NY: Harbrace.

4. Karlsen, C. (1987). *The devil in the shape of a woman: Witchcraft in colonial New England.* New York: Norton.

5. Putnam, A. (1881). *Witchcraft of New England explained by modern spiritualism.* Boston, MA: Colby & Rich.

6. Schoeneman, T. (1975). The witchhunt as a cultural change phenomena. *Ethos, 3*(4), 528-536.

7. Starkey, M. L. (1949). *The devil in Massachusetts: A modern inquiry into the Salem witch trials.* New York, NY: Knopf.

8. Levin, D. (1960). *What happened in Salem? Documents pertaining to the 17th Century witchcraft trials.* New York, NY: Harbrace.

9. Victor, J. (1992). The search for scapegoat deviants. *The Humanist, 52,* 10-13.

10. Boyer, P., & Nissenbaum, S. (1974). *Salem possessed: The social origins of witchcraft.* Cambridge, MA: Harvard University Press.

11. Boyer, P., & Nissenbaum, S. (1977). *The Salem witchcraft papers: A verbatim transcripts of the legal documents of the Salem witchcraft outbreak of 1692.* New York, NY: Da Capo Press.

12. Hall, D. (1991). *Witch-hunting in Seventeenth-Century New England: A documentary history, 1638-1692.* Boston, MA: Northeastern University Press.

13. Bailey, S. L. (1880). *Historical sketches of Andover.* Boston, MA: Knopf.

14. Klaits, J. (1984). *Servants of Satan: The age of the witch hunts.* Bloomfield, IN: University Press.

15. Levack, B. (1971). *The witch-hunts in early modern England.* New York, NY: Longman House.

16. Mather, C. (1950). *On witchcraft.* New York, NY: Peter Pauper Press.

17. Putnam, A. (1881). *Witchcraft of New England explained by modern spiritualism.* Boston, MA: Colby & Rich.

18. Robinson, E. A. (1991). *The Devil discovered: Salem witchcraft 1692.* New York, NY: Hippocrene Books.

19. Silverman, K. (1971). *Selected letters of Cotton Mather.* Baton Rouge, LA: Louisiana State University Press.

20. Victor, J. (1992). The search for scapegoat deviants. *The Humanist, 52,* 10-13.

21. Starkey, M. L. (1969). *The Devil in Massachusetts: A modern inquiry into the Salem witch trials.* New York, NY: Double Day.

22. Thomas, K. (1971). *Religion and the decline of magic: Studies in popular beliefs in sixteenth and seventeenth-century England.* London: Weidenfeld & Nicolson.

23. Sheets, R. N. (1992). Newman family newsletter. *Newman Family Historical Society, 127,* 1-37.

24. Calef, R. (1914). *More wonders of the invisible world*. New York, NY: Scribner.

25. Drake, S. (1869). *Annuals of witchcraft in New England: And elsewhere in the United States*. New York, NY: Benjamin Blom.

26. Hall, D. (1991). *Witch-hunting in Seventeenth-Century New England: A documentary history, 1638-1692*. Boston, MA: Northeastern University Press.

27. Miller, P. (1953). *The New England mind: From colony to providence*. Cambridge, MA: Harvard University Press.

28. Thomas, H. M. (1973). *The diary of Samuel Sewall, 1674-1729*. New York, NY: Farrar, Straus & Giroux.

29. Robinson, E. A. (1991). *The Devil discovered: Salem witchcraft 1692*. New York, NY: Hippocrene Books.

30. Silverman, K. (1971). *Selected letters of Cotton Mather*. Baton Rouge, LA: Louisiana State University Press.

31. Victor, J. (1992). The search for scapegoat deviants. *The Humanist, 52*, 10-13.

32. Starkey, M. L. (1969). *The Devil in Massachusetts: A modern inquiry into the Salem witch trials*. New York, NY: Double Day.

33. Thomas, K. (1971). *Religion and the decline of magic: Studies in popular beliefs in sixteenth and seventeenth-century England*. London: Weidenfeld & Nicolson.

CHAPTER FIVE REFERENCES

1. Thomas, K. (1971). *Religion and the decline of magic: Studies in popular beliefs in sixteenth and seventeenth-century England.* London: Weidenfeld & Nicolson.

2. Sheets, R. N. (1992). Newman family newsletter. *Newman Family Historical Society, 127,* 1-37.

3. Calef, R. (1914). *More wonders of the invisible world.* New York, NY: Scribner.

4. Drake, S. (1869). *Annuals of witchcraft in New England: And elsewhere in the United States.* New York, NY: Benjamin Blom.

5. Hall, D. (1991). *Witch-hunting in Seventeenth-Century New England: A documentary history, 1638-1692.* Boston, MA: Northeastern University Press.

6. Miller, P. (1953). *The New England mind: From colony to providence.* Cambridge, MA: Harvard University Press.

7. Thomas, H. M. (1973). *The diary of Samuel Sewall, 1674-1729.* New York, NY: Farrar, Straus & Giroux.

8. Robinson, E. A. (1991). *The Devil discovered: Salem witchcraft 1692.* New York, NY: Hippocrene Books.

9. Silverman, K. (1971). *Selected letters of Cotton Mather.* Baton Rouge, LA: Louisiana State University Press.

10. Victor, J. (1992). The search for scapegoat deviants. *The Humanist, 52*, 10-13.

11. Starkey, M. L. (1969). *The Devil in Massachusetts: A modern inquiry into the Salem witch trials.* New York, NY: Double Day.

12. Thomas, K. (1971). *Religion and the decline of magic: Studies in popular beliefs in sixteenth and seventeenth-century England.* London: Weidenfeld & Nicolson.

13. Boyer, P., & Nissenbaum, S. (1974). *Salem possessed: The social origins of witchcraft.* Cambridge, MA: Harvard University Press.

14. Boyer, P., & Nissenbaum, S. (1977). *The Salem witchcraft papers: A verbatim transcripts of the legal documents of the Salem witchcraft outbreak of 1692.* New York, NY: Da Capo Press.

15. Hall, D. (1991). *Witch-hunting in Seventeenth-Century New England: A documentary history, 1638-1692.* Boston, MA: Northeastern University Press.

16. Bailey, S. L. (1880). *Historical sketches of Andover.* Boston, MA: Knopf.

17. Klaits, J. (1984). *Servants of Satan: The age of the witch hunts.* Bloomfield, IN: University Press.

18. Levack, B. (1971). *The witch-hunts in early modern England.* New York, NY: Longman House.

19. Levin, D. (1960). *What happened in Salem? Documents pertaining to the 17th Century witchcraft trials.* New York, NY: Harbrace.

20. Karlsen, C. (1987). *The devil in the shape of a woman: Witchcraft in colonial New England.* New York: Norton.

21. Putnam, A. (1881). *Witchcraft of New England explained by modern spiritualism.* Boston, MA: Colby & Rich.

22. Schoeneman, T. (1975). The witchhunt as a cultural change phenomena. *Ethos, 3*(4), 528-536.

23. Hall, D. (1991). *Witch-hunting in Seventeenth-Century New England: A documentary history, 1638-1692*. Boston, MA: Northeastern University Press.

24. Bailey, S. L. (1880). *Historical sketches of Andover*. Boston, MA: Knopf.

25. Klaits, J. (1984). *Servants of Satan: The age of the witch hunts*. Bloomfield, IN: University Press.

26. Victor, J. (1992). The search for scapegoat deviants. *The Humanist, 52*, 10-13.

27. Starkey, M. L. (1969). *The Devil in Massachusetts: A modern inquiry into the Salem witch trials*. New York, NY: Double Day.

28. Thomas, K. (1971). *Religion and the decline of magic: Studies in popular beliefs in sixteenth and seventeenth-century England*. London: Weidenfeld & Nicolson.

29. Sheets, R. N. (1992). Newman family newsletter. *Newman Family Historical Society, 127*, 1-37.

30. Klaits, J. (1984). *Servants of Satan: The age of the witch hunts*. Bloomfield, IN: University Press.

31. Levack, B. (1971). *The witch-hunts in early modern England*. New York, NY: Longman House.

32. Mather, C. (1950). *On witchcraft*. New York, NY: Peter Pauper Press.

33. Mather, C. (1950). *On witchcraft*. New York, NY: Peter Pauper Press.

34. Levin, D. (1960). *What happened in Salem? Documents pertaining to the 17th Century witchcraft trials*. New York, NY: Harbrace.

35. Victor, J. (1992). The search for scapegoat deviants. *The Humanist, 52*, 10-13.

CHAPTER SIX REFERENCES

1. Boyer, P., & Nissenbaum, S. (1977). *The Salem witchcraft papers: A verbatim transcripts of the legal documents of the Salem witchcraft outbreak of 1692.* New York, NY: Da Capo Press.

2. Hall, D. (1991). *Witch-hunting in Seventeenth-Century New England: A documentary history, 1638-1692.* Boston, MA: Northeastern University Press.

3. Bailey, S. L. (1880). *Historical sketches of Andover.* Boston, MA: Knopf.

4. Klaits, J. (1984). *Servants of Satan: The age of the witch hunts.* Bloomfield, IN: University Press.

5. Levack, B. (1971). *The witch-hunts in early modern England.* New York, NY: Longman House.

6. Mather, C. (1950). *On witchcraft.* New York, NY: Peter Pauper Press.

7. Mather, C. (1950). *On witchcraft.* New York, NY: Peter Pauper Press.

8. Burr, G. L. (1975). *Narratives of the witchcraft cases, 1648-1706.* New York, NY: Scribner.

9. Marshall, R. (1995). *Witchcraft: The history and mythology.* New York, NY: Random House.

10. Levin, D. (1960). *What happened in Salem? Documents pertaining to the 17th Century witchcraft trials.* New York, NY: Harbrace.

11. Karlsen, C. (1987). *The devil in the shape of a woman: Witchcraft in colonial New England.* New York: Norton.

12. Starkey, M. L. (1949). *The devil in Massachusetts: A modern inquiry into the Salem witch trials.* New York, NY: Knopf.

13. Levin, D. (1960). *What happened in Salem? Documents pertaining to the 17th Century witchcraft trials.* New York, NY: Harbrace.

14. Victor, J. (1992). The search for scapegoat deviants. *The Humanist, 52*, 10-13.

15. Boyer, P., & Nissenbaum, S. (1977). *The Salem witchcraft papers: A verbatim transcripts of the legal documents of the Salem witchcraft outbreak of 1692.* New York, NY: Da Capo Press.

16. Hall, D. (1991). *Witch-hunting in Seventeenth-Century New England: A documentary history, 1638-1692.* Boston, MA: Northeastern University Press.

17. Levack, B. (1971). *The witch-hunts in early modern England.* New York, NY: Longman House.

18. Mather, C. (1950). *On witchcraft.* New York, NY: Peter Pauper Press.

19. Levin, D. (1960). *What happened in Salem? Documents pertaining to the 17th Century witchcraft trials.* New York, NY: Harbrace.

20. Mather, C. (1950). *On witchcraft.* New York, NY: Peter Pauper Press.

CHAPTER SEVEN REFERENCES

1. Putnam, A. (1881). *Witchcraft of New England explained by modern spiritualism.* Boston, MA: Colby & Rich.

2. Schoeneman, T. (1975). The witchhunt as a cultural change phenomena. *Ethos, 3*(4), 528-536.

3. Starkey, M. L. (1949). *The devil in Massachusetts: A modern inquiry into the Salem witch trials.* New York, NY: Knopf.

4. Levin, D. (1960). *What happened in Salem? Documents pertaining to the 17th Century witchcraft trials.* New York, NY: Harbrace.

5. Victor, J. (1992). The search for scapegoat deviants. *The Humanist, 52,* 10-13.

6. Boyer, P., & Nissenbaum, S. (1974). *Salem possessed: The social origins of witchcraft.* Cambridge, MA: Harvard University Press.

7. Boyer, P., & Nissenbaum, S. (1977). *The Salem witchcraft papers: A verbatim transcripts of the legal documents of the Salem witchcraft outbreak of 1692.* New York, NY: Da Capo Press.

8. Hall, D. (1991). *Witch-hunting in Seventeenth-Century New England: A documentary history, 1638-1692.* Boston, MA: Northeastern University Press.

9. Bailey, S. L. (1880). *Historical sketches of Andover.* Boston, MA: Knopf.

10. Klaits, J. (1984). *Servants of Satan: The age of the witch hunts.* Bloomfield, IN: University Press.

11. Levack, B. (1971). *The witch-hunts in early modern England.* New York, NY: Longman House.

12. Mather, C. (1950). *On witchcraft.* New York, NY: Peter Pauper Press.

13. Thomas, K. (1971). *Religion and the decline of magic: Studies in popular beliefs in sixteenth and seventeenth-century England.* London: Weidenfeld & Nicolson.

14. Sheets, R. N. (1992). Newman family newsletter. *Newman Family Historical Society, 127,* 1-37.

15. Calef, R. (1914). *More wonders of the invisible world.* New York, NY: Scribner.

16. Drake, S. (1869). *Annuals of witchcraft in New England: And elsewhere in the United States.* New York, NY: Benjamin Blom.

17. Hall, D. (1991). *Witch-hunting in Seventeenth-Century New England: A documentary history, 1638-1692.* Boston, MA: Northeastern University Press.

18. Miller, P. (1953). The *New England mind: From colony to providence.* Cambridge, MA: Harvard University Press.

19. Thomas, H. M. (1973). *The diary of Samuel Sewall, 1674-1729.* New York, NY: Farrar, Straus & Giroux.

20. Robinson, E. A. (1991). *The Devil discovered: Salem witchcraft 1692.* New York, NY: Hippocrene Books.

21. Silverman, K. (1971). *Selected letters of Cotton Mather.* Baton Rouge, LA: Louisiana State University Press.

22. Victor, J. (1992). The search for scapegoat deviants. *The Humanist, 52,* 10-13.

23. Starkey, M. L. (1969). *The Devil in Massachusetts: A modern inquiry into the Salem witch trials.* New York, NY: Double Day.

24. Burr, G. L. (1975). *Narratives of the witchcraft cases, 1648-1706.* New York, NY: Scribner.

25. Marshall, R. (1995). *Witchcraft: The history and mythology.* New York, NY: Random House.

26. Levin, D. (1960). *What happened in Salem? Documents pertaining to the 17th Century witchcraft trials.* New York, NY: Harbrace.

27. Karlsen, C. (1987). *The devil in the shape of a woman: Witchcraft in colonial New England.* New York: Norton.

28. Putnam, A. (1881). *Witchcraft of New England explained by modern spiritualism.* Boston, MA: Colby & Rich.

29. Schoeneman, T. (1975). *The witchhunt as a cultural change phenomena. Ethos, 3*(4), 528-536.

30. Starkey, M. L. (1949). *The devil in Massachusetts: A modern inquiry into the Salem witch trials.* New York, NY: Knopf.

31. Levin, D. (1960). *What happened in Salem? Documents pertaining to the 17th Century witchcraft trials.* New York, NY: Harbrace.

32. Victor, J. (1992). The search for scapegoat deviants. *The Humanist, 52,* 10-13.

33. Boyer, P., & Nissenbaum, S. (1974). *Salem possessed: The social origins of witchcraft.* Cambridge, MA: Harvard University Press.

34. Boyer, P., & Nissenbaum, S. (1977). *The Salem witchcraft papers: A verbatim transcripts of the legal documents of the Salem witchcraft outbreak of 1692.* New York, NY: Da Capo Press.

35. Hall, D. (1991). *Witch-hunting in Seventeenth-Century New England: A documentary history, 1638-1692.* Boston, MA: Northeastern University Press.

36. Bailey, S. L. (1880). *Historical sketches of Andover.* Boston, MA: Knopf.

37. Klaits, J. (1984). *Servants of Satan: The age of the witch hunts.* Bloomfield, IN: University Press.

38. Levack, B. (1971). *The witch-hunts in early modern England.* New York, NY: Longman House.

39. Mather, C. (1950). *On witchcraft.* New York, NY: Peter Pauper Press.

40. Klaits, J. (1984). *Servants of Satan: The age of the witch hunts.* Bloomfield, IN: University Press.

41. Levack, B. (1971). *The witch-hunts in early modern England.* New York, NY: Longman House.

42. Mather, C. (1950). *On witchcraft.* New York, NY: Peter Pauper Press.

43. Levin, D. (1960). *What happened in Salem? Documents pertaining to the 17th Century witchcraft trials.* New York, NY: Harbrace.

44. Karlsen, C. (1987). *The devil in the shape of a woman: Witchcraft in colonial New England.* New York: Norton.

45. Putnam, A. (1881). *Witchcraft of New England explained by modern spiritualism.* Boston, MA: Colby & Rich.

46. Schoeneman, T. (1975). *The witchhunt as a cultural change phenomena. Ethos, 3*(4), 528-536.

47. Starkey, M. L. (1949). *The devil in Massachusetts: A modern inquiry into the Salem witch trials.* New York, NY: Knopf.

48. Levin, D. (1960). *What happened in Salem? Documents pertaining to the 17th Century witchcraft trials.* New York, NY: Harbrace.

49. Victor, J. (1992). The search for scapegoat deviants. *The Humanist, 52,* 10-13.

50. Boyer, P., & Nissenbaum, S. (1974). *Salem possessed: The social origins of witchcraft*. Cambridge, MA: Harvard University Press.

51. Boyer, P., & Nissenbaum, S. (1977). *The Salem witchcraft papers: A verbatim transcripts of the legal documents of the Salem witchcraft outbreak of 1692*. New York, NY: Da Capo Press.

52. Boyer, P., & Nissenbaum, S. (1977). *The Salem witchcraft papers: A verbatim transcripts of the legal documents of the Salem witchcraft outbreak of 1692*. New York, NY: Da Capo Press.

53. Hall, D. (1991). *Witch-hunting in Seventeenth-Century New England: A documentary history, 1638-1692*. Boston, MA: Northeastern University Press.

54. Bailey, S. L. (1880). *Historical sketches of Andover*. Boston, MA: Knopf.

55. Klaits, J. (1984). *Servants of Satan: The age of the witch hunts*. Bloomfield, IN: University Press.

56. Levack, B. (1971). *The witch-hunts in early modern England*. New York, NY: Longman House.

57. Mather, C. (1950). *On witchcraft*. New York, NY: Peter Pauper Press.

58. Klaits, J. (1984). *Servants of Satan: The age of the witch hunts*. Bloomfield, IN: University Press.

59. Levack, B. (1971). *The witch-hunts in early modern England*. New York, NY: Longman House.

60. Mather, C. (1950). *On witchcraft*. New York, NY: Peter Pauper Press.

61. Levin, D. (1960). *What happened in Salem? Documents pertaining to the 17th Century witchcraft trials*. New York, NY: Harbrace.

62. Karlsen, C. (1987). *The devil in the shape of a woman: Witchcraft in colonial New England*. New York: Norton.

63. Putnam, A. (1881). *Witchcraft of New England explained by modern spiritualism*. Boston, MA: Colby & Rich.

64. Schoeneman, T. (1975). The witchhunt as a cultural change phenomena. *Ethos, 3*(4), 528-536.

65. Starkey, M. L. (1949). *The devil in Massachusetts: A modern inquiry into the Salem witch trials*. New York, NY: Knopf.

66. Levack, B. (1971). *The witch-hunts in early modern England*. New York, NY: Longman House.

67. Mather, C. (1950). *On witchcraft*. New York, NY: Peter Pauper Press.

68. Levack, B. (1971). *The witch-hunts in early modern England*. New York, NY: Longman House.

69. Mather, C. (1950). *On witchcraft*. New York, NY: Peter Pauper Press.

70. Hall, D. (1991). *Witch-hunting in Seventeenth-Century New England: A documentary history, 1638-1692*. Boston, MA: Northeastern University Press.

71. Bailey, S. L. (1880). *Historical sketches of Andover*. Boston, MA: Knopf.

72. Klaits, J. (1984). *Servants of Satan: The age of the witch hunts*. Bloomfield, IN: University Press.

73. Levack, B. (1971). *The witch-hunts in early modern England*. New York, NY: Longman House.

74. Mather, C. (1950). *On witchcraft*. New York, NY: Peter Pauper Press.

75. Putnam, A. (1881). *Witchcraft of New England explained by modern spiritualism*. Boston, MA: Colby & Rich.

76. Robinson, E. A. (1991). *The Devil discovered: Salem witchcraft 1692*. New York, NY: Hippocrene Books.

77. Silverman, K. (1971). *Selected letters of Cotton Mather.* Baton Rouge, LA: Louisiana State University Press.

78. Victor, J. (1992). The search for scapegoat deviants. *The Humanist, 52,* 10-13.

79. Starkey, M. L. (1969). *The Devil in Massachusetts: A modern inquiry into the Salem witch trials.* New York, NY: Double Day.

80. Thomas, K. (1971). *Religion and the decline of magic: Studies in popular beliefs in sixteenth and seventeenth-century England.* London: Weidenfeld & Nicolson.

81. Sheets, R. N. (1992). Newman family newsletter. *Newman Family Historical Society, 127,* 1-37.

82. Calef, R. (1914). *More wonders of the invisible world.* New York, NY: Scribner.

83. Drake, S. (1869). *Annuals of witchcraft in New England: And elsewhere in the United States.* New York, NY: Benjamin Blom.

84. Hall, D. (1991). *Witch-hunting in Seventeenth-Century New England: A documentary history, 1638-1692.* Boston, MA: Northeastern University Press.

85. Victor, J. (1992). The search for scapegoat deviants. *The Humanist, 52,* 10-13.

86. Starkey, M. L. (1969). *The Devil in Massachusetts: A modern inquiry into the Salem witch trials.* New York, NY: Double Day.

87. Thomas, K. (1971). *Religion and the decline of magic: Studies in popular beliefs in sixteenth and seventeenth-century England.* London: Weidenfeld & Nicolson.

88. Levack, B. (1971). *The witch-hunts in early modern England.* New York, NY: Longman House.

89. Mather, C. (1950). *On witchcraft.* New York, NY: Peter Pauper Press.

90. Klaits, J. (1984). *Servants of Satan: The age of the witch hunts*. Bloomfield, IN: University Press.

91. Boyer, P., & Nissenbaum, S. (1974). *Salem possessed: The social origins of witchcraft*. Cambridge, MA: Harvard University Press.

92. Boyer, P., & Nissenbaum, S. (1977). *The Salem witchcraft papers: A verbatim transcripts of the legal documents of the Salem witchcraft outbreak of 1692*. New York, NY: Da Capo Press.

93. Mather, C. (1950). *On witchcraft*. New York, NY: Peter Pauper Press.

94. Putnam, A. (1881). *Witchcraft of New England explained by modern spiritualism*. Boston, MA: Colby & Rich.

95. Robinson, E. A. (1991). *The Devil discovered: Salem witchcraft 1692*. New York, NY: Hippocrene Books.

96. Mather, C. (1950). *On witchcraft*. New York, NY: Peter Pauper Press.

97. Robinson, E. A. (1991). *The Devil discovered: Salem witchcraft 1692*. New York, NY: Hippocrene Books.

CHAPTER EIGHT REFERENCES

1. Marshall, R. (1995). *Witchcraft: The history and mythology.* New York, NY: Random House.

2. Levin, D. (1960). *What happened in Salem? Documents pertaining to the 17th Century witchcraft trials.* New York, NY: Harbrace.

3. Karlsen, C. (1987). *The devil in the shape of a woman: Witchcraft in colonial New England.* New York: Norton.

4. Putnam, A. (1881). *Witchcraft of New England explained by modern spiritualism.* Boston, MA: Colby & Rich.

5. Boyer, P., & Nissenbaum, S. (1977). *The Salem witchcraft papers: A verbatim transcripts of the legal documents of the Salem witchcraft outbreak of 1692.* New York, NY: Da Capo Press.

6. Robinson, E. A. (1991). *The Devil discovered: Salem witchcraft 1692.* New York, NY: Hippocrene Books.

7. Starkey, M. L. (1969). *The Devil in Massachusetts: A modern inquiry into the Salem witch trials.* New York, NY: Double Day.

8. Sheets, R. N. (1992). Newman family newsletter. *Newman Family Historical Society, 127,* 1-37.

9. Putnam, A. (1881). *Witchcraft of New England explained by modern spiritualism.* Boston, MA: Colby & Rich.

10. Upham, C. (1959). *Salem witchcraft: With an account of Salem village and a history of opinions on witchcraft and kindred subjects.* New York, NY: Frederick Ungar Publishing Company.

11. Boyer, P., & Nissenbaum, S. (1977). *The Salem witchcraft papers: A verbatim transcripts of the legal documents of the Salem witchcraft outbreak of 1692.* New York, NY: Da Capo Press.

12. Klaits, J. (1984). *Servants of Satan: The age of the witch hunts.* Bloomfield, IN: University Press.

www.ingramcontent.com/pod-product-compliance
Lightning Source LLC
Chambersburg PA
CBHW021017180526
45163CB00005B/1997